"This is the perfect biography of C.S. L ...
who read this biography will not only ...
will know in their bones what it *felt like* to be the man whose dreams of
lions led to the creation of Narnia."

WALTER HOOPER
Author of *C.S. Lewis: A Complete Guide to His Life & Works*
Literary Adviser to the Estate of C.S. Lewis

"Will Vaus has crafted a wise and winsome book sure to delight readers of
all ages; Professor Lewis would be pleased indeed."

DR. BRUCE EDWARDS
Editor of *C.S. Lewis: Life, Works and Legacy* (Praeger, 2007)
Professor of English and Africana Studies, Bowling Green State University

"With all the definitive biographies written on C.S. Lewis, finally there is
one that will appeal to all the young readers of *The Chronicles*. Will Vaus
has written Lewis's story interspersed with incidents from *The Chronicles*
with just the right touch to answer all their youthful curiosity, and that
includes the young in heart also."

DR. CLARA SARROCCO
Secretary, The New York C.S. Lewis Society

"A true Narnian and C.S. Lewis scholar, Will Vaus will delight everyone
who reads *The Professor of Narnia*. From Ireland to England to Greece and
more, readers will journey through the fascinating life of C.S. Lewis with
Vaus as the knowledgeable, endearing, and captivating tour guide."

ROBERT VELARDE
Author of *Conversations with C.S. Lewis* and *The Heart of Narnia*

"Vaus weaves together the wonder Lewis discovers about the world with the
biographical details that form him as the beloved author of Narnia. This

book will be the spark for many young readers that will light up their imaginations about the professor that wrote for them."

ZACH KINCAID
Editor of the CSLewis.com blog
Director of The Matthew's House Project (www.matthewshouse.net)

"*The Professor of Narnia* presents the remarkable and inspiring, true story of C.S. Lewis, the most important and influential Christian writer of modern times. This charming and insightful book guides the reader through Lewis's life, ideas, and bountiful work and explains how one of the greatest scholars of the 20th Century came to faith and then lived a life of service, humility, insight, wit, and immense impact worldwide. This book will enrich everyone, including the young reader, who has come to love *The Chronicles of Narnia*, and has wondered about its origin, meaning and author."

DAVID J. THEROUX
President, C.S. Lewis Society of California
President, The Independent Institute

"The Professor of Narnia provides a coherent overview of the life of C.S. Lewis for younger readers, and will also be of use to older enthusiasts who will appreciate this thoughtful and chronological retelling of Jack's story set against the background of the Narnian tales."

DAN HAMILTON
Author of the *Tales of the Forgotten God* trilogy
Co-author of *In Pursuit of C.S. Lewis*

THE
PROFESSOR
OF
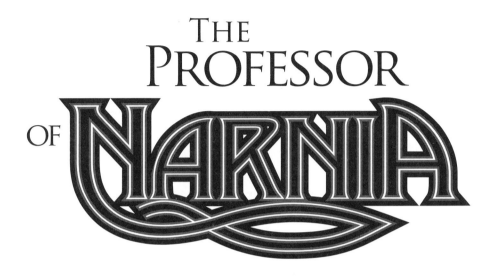

THE
PROFESSOR
OF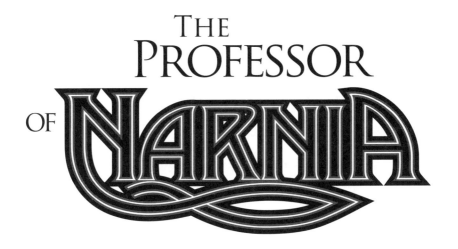

Will Vaus

BELIEVE BOOKS
Life Stories That Inspire
WASHINGTON, DC

THE PROFESSOR OF NARNIA
By Will Vaus

Scripture taken from the HOLY BIBLE, NEW INTERNATIONAL VERSION®.
Copyright © 1973, 1978, 1984 International Bible Society. Used by permission of
Zondervan. All rights reserved.

The "NIV" and "New International Version" trademarks are registered in the
United States Patent and Trademark Office by International Bible Society. Use of
either trademark requires the permission of International Bible Society.

Cover photo by Burt Glinn, used by permission of Magnum Photos.
Photos of C.S. Lewis, family & friends used by permission of The Marion E.
Wade Center, Wheaton College, Wheaton, IL.
All other photos courtesy of the author.

ISBN: 0-9817061-0-X
Library of Congress Control Number: 2008935521

Cover design: *Jack Kotowicz, Washington, DC, VelocityDesignGroup.com*
Layout design: *Annie Kotowicz, AnnieKotowicz.com*

Believe Books publishes the inspirational life stories of extraordinary believers in
God from around the world. Requests for information should be addressed to
Believe Books at www.believebooks.com. **Believe Books** is a registered trade name
of **Believe Books, LLC** of Washington, DC.

Printed in the United States of America

For James, Jonathan & Joshua
True Friends of Narnia

CONTENTS

FOREWORD

This is the perfect biography of C.S. Lewis for children. I like it so much that I'm going to go out on a limb and say something daring. If Lewis were alive today and if author Will Vaus were to ask his opinion of this book, I believe that first of all, Lewis would scold Will for not having chosen a more worthy subject. Secondly, after the scolding, I think Lewis would thank the author for giving him his rightful place in history—*not* as a writer of current times, but as an Irishman living in England during the first part of the 20th century.

That is a *very* important difference. One of the key principles of Lewis's years of teaching literary history was that it is essential that an author be placed in the actual historical context in which he lived. If you treat an author who lived a long time ago as if he were almost exactly like yourself —as if writing with a dip pen was much the same as using a computer and an Oxford College 550 years old almost the same as an American university 20 years old—the subject of your biography will be mainly imaginary.

And if the subject of the biography is imaginary, you learn nothing from the book. No. The right way, the honest way, is the one Lewis followed in his literary studies.

First of all, he believed that if a writer smudges over the differences between various periods he is causing us to be "disinherited" of what we need, and want, to know. Secondly, Lewis believed that to enjoy "full humanity" we ought, so far as possible, to "become an Achaean chief while reading Homer, a medieval knight while reading Malory, and an eighteenth-century Londoner while reading Johnson. Only thus will you be able to judge the work 'in the same spirit that its author writ' and to avoid chimerical criticism."*

I'm not sure I've read a biography of Lewis in which this ideal has been realized as well as it is here. Dare I confess it? When I first picked it up I was afraid that if Will Vaus mentioned Lewis's method of writing he would bewail the fact that Lewis did not have computers, email, laser printers and the rest. I need not have feared. This author has more than done his 'homework' and there is a fine passage on pages 11–12 explaining how Lewis wrote. Indeed, on almost every page there are descriptions of how things appeared to Lewis. I give Will Vaus as many stars as you like because the boys and girls who read this biography will not only know how Lewis spent his time, but will know in their bones what it *felt like* to be the man whose dreams of lions led to the creation of Narnia.

WALTER HOOPER
Author of *C.S. Lewis: A Complete Guide to His Life & Works*
Literary Adviser to the Estate of C.S. Lewis
Oxford, England

---

* C.S. Lewis, *A Preface to Paradise Lost* (London: Oxford University Press, 1942), ch. IX, p. 63.

INTRODUCTION

Our story begins when I was nine years old. I was living in Southern California with my family. I was in the fourth grade in public school, and that year I had the great blessing of having one of the most wonderful teachers in the world. Her name was Mrs. Ewing. She was a fantastic teacher for any number of reasons. I remember at Christmas time she would decorate our classroom with a Christmas tree, a hand-painted nativity scene atop a bookshelf and popcorn strings hanging from the ceiling.

Mrs. Ewing was the first person to teach me how to write. I had been writing and illustrating my own unpublished stories since I was very young. However, Mrs. Ewing taught me how to really write by giving me a big assignment: the writing of my autobiography! Though a child of nine, it seemed such a difficult task to write up my whole life story. I still have the book; it consists of twenty-one chapters, handwritten in cursive on sixty-four half-pages of newsprint, bound in decorated cardboard. On the first page is written in pencil: "A book to be proud of. Mrs. E."

Mrs. E could be tough as well as kind. I remember each day when we came in from recess we had to stand in a perfectly straight line outside her classroom door. Mrs. E would rattle off some mathematical equation and the first person to give the right answer would have the honor of being the first person to enter the classroom and take his or her seat. Mrs. E would continue shouting out equations for us to complete until everyone had given a correct answer. I, however, often had the sad distinction of being the last person to give the right answer to an equation. Though Mrs. E persisted in her attempts to make me a more expert mathematician, I liked her anyway.

Of all the wonderful things that Mrs. E did for our class, the best thing she ever did was to introduce us to a whole new world. Every day in class she would read to us a chapter from some sort of storybook. And so one day Mrs. E opened a book and began to read aloud to the class: "Once there were four children whose names were Peter, Susan, Edmund and Lucy." By the end of the first chapter of *The Lion, the Witch and the Wardrobe*, I was enchanted. My parents had never read any fantasy books to me when I was growing up and so, up until that day in Mrs. E's class, I had never chosen to read a fairy tale for myself.

I think, at first, I was enchanted with C.S. Lewis's description of winter itself, after Lucy enters the snowy wonderland of Narnia through the wardrobe door. In New York, where I had lived till age seven, it snowed a lot, but we had moved to California where I missed winter; I missed white Christmases. *The Lion, the Witch and the Wardrobe* reminded me just how magical winter could be.

I learned, years later, that C.S. Lewis was entranced with winter, just as I was. He lived in the British Isles where it doesn't snow very often, or even very much when it does snow. And so I think he longed for snowfall just as much as I did as a New York refugee transplanted to desert-like Southern California. Lewis's love of winter is portrayed in a letter he wrote to a young correspondent in 1955: "We had our first frost last night—this morning the lawns are all grey, with a pale, bright sunshine on them: wonderfully beautiful. And somehow exciting. The first beginning of the winter always excites me: it makes me want adventures."[1]

Lewis shared with me this magical sense of wintertime adventure through the opening chapters of *The Lion, the Witch and the Wardrobe*. His words cast a spell over me and thus I was transported into the even deeper magic of Narnia itself. I fell in love with Mr. Tumnus the Faun, the Beavers and, of course, the great lion, Aslan.

---

1. Walter Hooper, *The Collected Letters of C.S. Lewis*, Volume III, New York: HarperCollins, 2007, p. 659.

The Lion was the only one of The Chronicles of Narnia that Mrs. E read to our class, but by the end of her reading of that book, I was hooked. I felt I just had to read the rest of the series. And so, at my insistence, my parents bought me the boxed set of The Chronicles of Narnia. I still have those treasured, dog-eared, paperback copies, with black and white drawings by Pauline Baynes. I was a slow reader, but gradually I devoured all seven books. Prince Caspian was perhaps my favorite at first—partly because of the battle scene where a Telmarine head gets walloped off. I think every nine-year-old boy loves a good battle with knights in shining armor!

I don't remember when some of the Christian meaning in The Chronicles first became clear to me. I'm sure that, at first, I just loved the books because they were wonderful stories. There was no obvious connection for me between Narnia and the Bible. At that time in my life I found Sunday school and church, the few times I attended, to be boring beyond belief. And so nothing could have been further removed in my mind from the adventure of Narnia than the tedium of church. Eventually I did start attending church more regularly, once I began a personal relationship with Jesus Christ, but that is a story for another day and another book. What is important for you to know now is that when I was in high school, I had a very wise youth pastor whose name was Sonny Salsbury. Sonny challenged all of us in youth group not only to read the Bible but to read other Christian books as well. Among the books he encouraged us to read were the adult fiction and nonfiction works of C.S. Lewis. So I began to read more literature written by this man whose land of Narnia I had come to love.

From the time I was a small child, looking through a hand-held slide viewer at my parents' photographs of the changing of the guard at Buckingham Palace, or staring at the giant photos of the river Thames in our massive Time-Life Atlas, the far-away land of England had intrigued me. My parents took me on a trip to London when I was ten and I remember thinking, as I stared through the gates of the Queen's palace on a moonlit summer night, "This place is like something out of a C.S. Lewis book." I became then, if not before, what is called an Anglophile, a lover of England and all things English.

Thus, when I was in college and living on my own, master of my own schedule, at least during the summer months, I longed to travel to England again. My father graciously made that possible by paying for my trip; and so I traveled by myself to England and Ireland, with the special purpose in mind of visiting the places where C.S. Lewis lived, worked and worshiped. I took along with me all the Lewis books I had not yet read; I carried the books and all my clothes in a very heavy garment bag slung over my shoulder.

I flew from Los Angeles to London where I spent a week in a bed-and-breakfast hotel. From London it was on to Oxford where C.S. Lewis spent most of his life. From Oxford I trekked to Cambridge where Lewis was a professor toward the end of his earthly journey. I even went to visit some of Lewis's favorite haunts in Ireland. On the ferry ride from England, I read Lewis's novel *Till We Have Faces*, while sitting on the outside deck of the ship on a bright summer day with the sunlight glinting off the whitecaps of the Irish Sea.

And I will never forget reading *Mere Christianity* in a very small bed-and-breakfast hotel room in Lewis's beloved Donegal. It was raining cats and dogs outside my window and I was huddled in my tiny bed with a hundred-horsepower head cold! Once back in London, I picked up some new hardback copies of *The Chronicles* and began to read them again for the umpteenth time. C.S. Lewis often said that the sign of a good book was being able to read it many times over with growing delight. As many readers have discovered, that is certainly true of the Narnia books.

Over the years since college, I have actually read *The Chronicles of Narnia* more times than I can remember. I have formed C.S. Lewis book clubs in various places where I have lived just to have other people to talk with about Narnia! Desiring to learn more about the man, C.S. Lewis, I have, through the years, sought out a number of people who knew him. This very purposeful quest led to an e-mail correspondence with Lewis's stepson, Douglas Gresham. Those e-mails led me to conduct a C.S. Lewis tour of England during which Doug led our tour group around Oxford for three days. Discussions of C.S. Lewis and his books led to writing about Lewis and then eventually to the publication of my first book, *Mere Theology: A*

Guide to the Thought of C.S. Lewis. To top it all off, my wife and children joined me as I spent eight months working for Douglas Gresham and living in a house in Ireland known as The Narnia Cottage. During those eight months, I read all seven of *The Chronicles* aloud to my three sons (James, Jonathan and Joshua) who were 11, 9 and 5 years old at the time.

As I look back over a lifetime of reading books by and about C.S. Lewis, I wish that after I first read *The Chronicles of Narnia* there had been a simple biography I could have read that would have told me more about the professor behind Narnia, C.S. Lewis himself. That is why I am writing this book now. I am writing it for you because you, like me, may have enjoyed Narnia so much that you want to learn more about the man who wrote these fantastic books. Maybe you are an elementary school or middle school student. Or maybe you are a high school or college student like I was. Perhaps you are searching for the answers to intellectual questions you have about Christianity and you would like to learn more about the faith of the man behind Narnia. Or perhaps you are a parent whose children have fallen in love with the Narnia books and you want to get to know the author, C.S. Lewis, for yourself. Whatever stage of life in which you find yourself, I trust you will find something of interest in this book. And so, now that you have gotten to know a little bit about me, the author, we shall move on to a more important matter: the life story of C.S. Lewis.

Before we do that, I invite you to put on your "Narnia glasses" because we are going to look at the life of C.S. Lewis through those spectacles. There are so many themes, events and characters in Narnia which match the life of its author that looking at C.S. Lewis through the lens of Narnia just seemed natural to me. I hope you will agree and that you will enjoy getting to know the Professor of Narnia as you turn each page of this book.

1

A Boy Called Jack

In 1954, a group of fifth graders from Maryland wrote to C.S. Lewis to thank him for his Narnia books and ask him questions about the stories and himself. One question they must have had was: "What do you look and sound like?" C.S. Lewis's answer was: "I'm tall, fat, rather bald, red-faced, double-chinned, black-haired, have a deep voice, and wear glasses for reading."[2] That is how C.S. Lewis described himself around the time he was writing the following words. ...

> This is a story about something that happened long ago when your grand-father was a child. It is a very important story because it shows how all the comings and goings between our own world and the land of Narnia first began.
>
> In those days Mr. Sherlock Holmes was still living in Baker Street and the Bastables were looking for treasure in the Lewisham Road. In those days, if you were a boy you had to wear a stiff Eton collar every day, and schools were usually nastier than now. But meals were nicer; and as for sweets, I won't tell you how cheap and good they were, because it would only make your mouth water in vain.[3]

2. C.S. Lewis, *Letters to Children*, New York: Macmillan, 1985, p. 45.

3. C.S. Lewis, *The Magician's Nephew*, New York: HarperCollins, 1994, chapter 1, p. 3.

Thus begins *The Magician's Nephew*, a story set in the time period of C.S. Lewis's own childhood. The stories of Sherlock Holmes had first appeared in print in 1887. The Bastables were a middle-class family in E. Nesbit's *The Story of the Treasure Seekers*, published in 1898, the same year that Clive Staples Lewis was born in Belfast, Northern Ireland.

Clive was born on the cold and foggy afternoon of November 29 in a part of Belfast known as Strandtown, in one of a pair of semi-detached houses known as Dundela Villas. (A semi-detached house is one which shares one wall with another house.) The house in which Clive was born was torn down in 1952 and a group of rather drab flats (what Americans call apartments) now stand on the site. Though the house is no longer in existence, there is a plaque on the site which reads:

> C.S. Lewis
> 1898 – 1963
> Author and
> Christian apologist
> born
> on this site

An apologist is one who gives an apology, or a defense, for something. As you will soon learn, Clive grew up to be a great defender of the Christian faith. But we are getting ahead of ourselves.

FAMILY

Clive was the second son of Albert and Flora Lewis. Albert was a police court solicitor, or what Americans would call a lawyer. One thing that made Albert a great lawyer was the fact that he was a superb speaker, especially when it came to telling stories. Albert's great-grandfather was a Welsh farmer and his grandfather was a Methodist minister in Saltney; perhaps Albert and his son Clive both inherited their public speaking ability from Albert's grandfather. Albert's father was a shipyard worker in Merseyside, England who moved to Cork, in southern Ireland, and became a boilermaker in a shipyard. In 1868, five years after Albert's birth, the family moved to Belfast, the busy, shipbuilding city of Northern Ireland.

Clive's mother, Flora, was also a very intelligent person, but her abilities lay in a different arena. Flora earned top grades in geometry, algebra, logic and mathematics from Queen's College, Belfast. For some strange reason, Flora's ability in mathematics was never passed down to Clive and, in fact, this loss almost led to a great disaster in C.S. Lewis's life. (We will learn more about that later.)

For now, it is enough to tell you that both of Clive's parents loved books, especially books written by some of the great Victorian novelists. However, curiously enough, neither of Clive's parents had an interest in the type of books which would win his own admiration as soon as he could choose for himself what books he most enjoyed reading. Neither Flora nor Albert showed any interest in romantic poetry, and especially not in fairy tales.

Clive had only one sibling, his brother Warren, whom he called Warnie. Warnie was just three years older than Clive. Clive regarded Warnie as one of the greatest blessings of his childhood—along with his beloved nurse, Lizzie Endicott. Lizzie shared with the Lewis boys some of the wonderful Irish legends, like the story of Fionn and Una and the great giant Angus from Scotland. For those of you who do not know the story, it was Fionn who, according to legend, built the famous Giant's Causeway along the Antrim Coast north of Belfast, a place that C.S. Lewis often saw during his childhood.

The landscape of Ireland informed much of what C.S. Lewis would later put into his descriptions of the land of Narnia. One place Lewis often saw during his childhood was not far from the Giant's Causeway. These were the ruins of Dunluce Castle, perched prettily on a cliff descending to the waves of the sea. As you might guess, Dunluce planted a picture in Lewis's mind that would later bear fruit in the imaginative creation of Cair Paravel, especially the ruins of Cair Paravel as described in *Prince Caspian*.

Something else the young Lewis must often have seen dotting the landscape of his homeland were Dolmens. Dolmens are constructed out of rocks with one very large rock looking like a tabletop; smaller rocks underneath would support it. Dolmens were ancient tombs. In one of the Celtic languages, "Dolmen" means "stone table." It must have been the sight of one of these Dolmens that gave Lewis the mental picture for the Stone Table in the Narnia stories.

The stories told by Lizzie Endicott did much to fire the imagination of both Lewis brothers. When Clive and Warren heard about the pot of gold at the end of the rainbow and saw a rainbow outside their house one day, they decided to dig for gold in the garden. Of course, they didn't find any. But when their father, Albert, came home from work, he fell into the hole his sons had dug! As you can imagine, Albert was none too pleased.

CHURCH

Two months to the day after Clive was born, he was baptized by his maternal grandfather, the Reverend Thomas Hamilton, Rector (or pastor) of St. Mark's Church, Dundela. St. Mark's has been a much-loved place of worship ever since the foundation stone was laid in 1876 and the building was completed in 1891. The church is built of red sandstone and is the only church in Ireland designed by the English architect William Butterfield. Butterfield also designed Keble College, Oxford, where C.S. Lewis would later spend an important time in his life. If you ever get to visit both St. Mark's and Keble College, you will see the similarity between the two. The 150-foot-high bell tower of St. Mark's can be seen from miles around and thus is an area landmark.

C.S. Lewis's grandfather, Thomas, was the first Rector of St. Mark's; Clive's father, Albert, was a devoted member of the church who served at one time as both Churchwarden and Sunday School Superintendent. The silver vessels which are still used for Holy Communion were given to the church by Albert and his siblings. One thing you will want to be sure to see, if ever you do visit St. Mark's, is the beautiful stained glass window given to the church by C.S. Lewis and his brother Warren in honor of their father and mother. The Lewis window is in the nave (the main part of the church where the congregation sits) toward the back, along the right-hand side as you face the altar. However, C.S. Lewis and his family sat at the front of the nave near the pulpit where young Clive would have been under the watchful eye of the preacher.

Though the church was a regular part of young Clive's life, he did not consider himself a particularly religious boy. He would later write of these early years: "I was taught the usual things and made to say my prayers and in due time taken to church. I naturally accepted what I was told but I cannot remember feeling much interest in it."[4]

STORIES AND BEAUTY

The one thing Clive did take a strong interest in, from a young age, was drawing, and later writing stories about the pictures he had drawn. Clive's earliest interest was in what he and his brother both called "dressed animals." By this they meant the kind of animals one finds in the Beatrix Potter books. Potter's animals wear clothes and speak and act, at least toward one another, as human beings do toward each other. From a very early age, Clive had a special talent for being able to draw animals and other figures as though they were really moving. If you have ever tried to draw such a picture yourself, you will know how difficult a thing that is to do.

In spite of this early imaginative and creative ability displayed in drawing, one thing which was almost completely absent from Clive's early life was beauty. Clive was not aware of any beautiful picture on the walls of his parents' house, nor was he aware of any beautiful buildings in his neighborhood. I say that beauty was *almost* completely absent from Clive's life

---

4. C.S. Lewis, *Surprised by Joy*, New York: Harcourt, Brace Jovanovich, 1955, chapter 1, p. 7.

because beauty soon began to introduce itself. The first introduction of beauty into Clive's life came in an unusual way.

One day Clive's brother Warren fashioned a toy garden out of twigs and flowers on the lid of a biscuit tin, or what Americans would call a canister for cookies. To Clive, this toy garden was the first beauty he ever knew. Years later, Clive Staples Lewis would write much about Paradise, or Heaven, but much of what he wrote, imaginatively speaking, owed its inspiration to Warren's model garden on the lid of that biscuit tin.

Another source of beauty for young Clive came through the window of his nursery at Dundela Villas. From that window he and his brother could see what they called "the Green Hills," that is, the Castlereagh Hills of Northern Ireland. These hills were not very far away, but to children growing up in the days before automobiles, those hills seemed almost unreachable. Thus, as little Clive would look out his nursery window, the sight of those green hills filled him with a great sense of longing. The only way you will truly understand this feeling is if you have experienced it yourself. Perhaps, when looking at a picture in a book, or reading a story, or looking at a beautiful landscape, you longed to jump into that picture, become part of that story, or enter that landscape. That is what Clive felt as he gazed out of his nursery window at the Green Hills; he had a deep desire to go galloping across those hills. This experience of longing became very important in his life, as we shall soon see.

A NEW NAME

Young Clive was definitely a boy of strong likes and dislikes and he had a way of making his desires known to those in his family. One striking incident from his first years makes this quality quite clear, but first I must set the scene for you.

Every summer, Flora would take her boys on a month-long holiday to the sea, usually to some place along the Antrim coast north of Belfast like

Ballycastle or Castlerock. A trip to the seaside was a major event in those days. First, the boys would select all the toys and other things they wanted to take with them and then their mother would pack their bags. Next, there came the trip in a horse-drawn carriage to the railroad station, followed by a steam engine train ride, and concluding with the first breathtaking view of the ocean breakers and smell of the salt sea at their final destination.

Albert would seldom join his family on holiday because he could never stand to be away from his police court work for very long. Albert just didn't know what to do with himself on vacation; even if he did join the rest of his family for a day out, he would usually spend it pacing up and down the beach.

At any rate, it was during one of these seaside holidays that Clive suddenly came up to his mother one day and, pointing to himself, said, "He is Jacksie!" Obviously, by the age of four, Clive had come to the point where he thought that the baby names by which he had previously been called (Babs, Babbins and the like) were beneath him. From that point on, the young Clive refused to answer to any other name and so Jacksie it was. This was later shortened to Jacks and finally to Jack. And so I shall refer to Clive Staples Lewis as Jack for the rest of this book, for so he was known to his friends and family for the rest of his life.

Before leaving the topic of Jack's chosen name, you should be aware that two slightly different stories have been told about how C.S. Lewis chose Jacksie for his own nickname. The first story I heard from a second cousin of C.S. Lewis: Back in the days when Clive was growing up in Belfast, the city used to have trams that would trundle along the streets, taking people wherever they wanted to go in town. Horse-drawn trams were replaced by electric trams in the early part of the twentieth century. Apparently, young Clive had a favorite tram car conductor whose name was Jacksie. Clive was so taken with the tram and this particular conductor that he adopted the man's name as his own.

The other version of the story was told to me by my friend, Douglas Gresham, the stepson of C.S. Lewis, who comes into the latter part of our story. According to Doug, Jacksie was the name of a small dog that

Clive was fond of. The dog was run over, perhaps by the tram, and that is when Clive adopted the dog's name and thereafter refused to answer to any other name. Whichever version of the story is most accurate, one thing is clear: Jacksie had a mind of his own, even at a very young age, and he was very determined.

2

DIGORY AND HIS DYING MOTHER

The first big change in Jack's life happened at the age of seven when his family moved to a new house. In 1905, the Lewises moved from Dundela Villas to a house Jack's father had built further out from the city of Belfast. The house that the Lewises later named "Little Lea" was a large one by most people's standards. It was afforded, no doubt, by his father's growing and successful work as a lawyer. Jack wrote of this house: "I am a product of long corridors, empty sunlit rooms, upstairs indoor silences, attics explored in solitude, distant noises of gurgling cisterns and pipes, and the noise of wind under the tiles."[5]

What I find most interesting about this statement is what it reveals about a curious quirk of the human mind. You, too, will discover this quirk once you are grown up, for I have experienced it just as Jack and many other people have. I, too, like Jack, grew up in a large house, large enough for my parents and my four siblings and me to each have our own bedroom. Just as Jack wrote of Little Lea, so, too, I would have said about my childhood home: "It had long corridors." In fact, all the rooms seemed of immense size to me as a child. But on the occasions when I have been back to visit that house as an adult, I have realized that the same house is not nearly as large in reality as it was in my imagination. Why is that? That is the case because, as a child, one is smaller and so the world and everything in it

---

5. *Surprised by Joy*, chapter 1, p. 10.

seems larger than it does to an adult who is naturally taller, and to whom things like houses and rooms and corridors seem smaller.

Not only does our perception of space change when we grow up—so does our perception of time. I remember when I was a child wondering if I would ever grow up—adulthood seemed light-years away and every day seemed to progress so slowly, especially when I was waiting for my birthday or for Christmas to arrive. Now that I am grown up, the years seem to pass with lightning speed. Why? It is, once again, because my perspective has changed. When I was seven, a year represented one-seventh of my life. Now that I am forty-five, a year represents only one forty-fifth of my life. Each year now is a much smaller proportion of the whole and so it passes more quickly. So if you just can't wait to grow up, don't worry, it will happen sooner than you think!

As an adult, Jack loved thinking about these different perspectives on time and space. I'm sure you noticed in the Narnia books that time passes at a different rate of speed in Narnia than it does in our world. And curious things happen in certain spaces in C.S. Lewis's fairy tales. In one book, all of Narnia seems to be contained inside a wardrobe. And in another book, a new Narnia seems contained inside a stable in old Narnia! I think Jack wanted his readers to realize that time and space are not always what they appear to be.

And so I must tell you that Little Lea, while it was and is a large house, was not and is not, in reality, nearly as large as it was in Jack's childhood imagination. I have walked the corridors of Little Lea and they are not long at all. But to seven-year old Jack, his new house probably seemed like a whole new world.

Jack's "big" new house was also filled with a seemingly endless supply of books. You will remember that Albert and Flora were both great readers, and they taught their children to be eager readers as well. Flora read good books to her sons and, when Jack and Warnie were old enough to read for themselves, they were allowed to read any book in the house.

Jack and Warnie also had plenty of time on their hands to read. That is because of two things. First of all, it rains a lot in Belfast. Secondly, when Jack and Warnie were growing up, parents were afraid of their children getting seriously ill if they were allowed to play outside in damp weather. Thus there were many days when the young Lewis boys were kept indoors.

THE LITTLE END ROOM

The Lewis boys filled their indoor hours not only with reading but also, as I mentioned earlier, with writing their own stories. It was in the upstairs "Little End Room" at Little Lea that Jack began writing and illustrating his first tales. What drove Jack to be a writer was a deformed thumb; Jack and Warnie each had only one joint in their thumbs, a trait inherited from their father. Thus Jack could not ever really make much of anything with his hands. This inability to create physical objects drove him to create imaginary worlds through words and pictures.

The third floor of Little Lea was Jack and Warnie's territory. The two main rooms at either end of that third floor were relatively small compared to the other rooms of the house and were decreased significantly in size by the slant of the roof. An adult visiting Jack and Warnie's rooms would have to be careful where he or she was standing in those rooms because they might easily knock their head against the ceiling!

From the room at one end of the house, Jack and Warnie could look out and see, not too far away, the tower of St. Mark's Church. Beyond that there was Belfast Lough with its massive shipyard—where the great ship Titanic was built beginning in 1909. And even further beyond that, Jack and Warnie could spy the Antrim Mountains in the misty distance. From the Little End Room on the other side of the house, Jack and Warnie could look out to their beloved Holywood Hills where they enjoyed bicycling together in good weather.

It was in the Little End Room that Jack kept his pen and inkpot. Jack wrote all his stories, throughout his entire life, with pen and ink. If you have never seen it done, a nib pen is dipped into a bottle of ink and then, with that ink on the nib, one can write a few words. Then one has to pause and dip the pen into the ink again before continuing. Jack came to love writing in this manner because every time he had to pause to dip his pen into the ink, it gave him time to think about what he wanted to write next. In addition to pen and inkpot, Jack kept his writing books and paint box in the Little End Room.

One interesting feature of the Little End Room is that it had a small door along one side, opening onto a crawl space, or attic, immediately under the roof of Little Lea. As a little boy, Jack liked to play in "his" attic. Perhaps this is where he got the idea, many years later, for what he would write about Polly's play attic in *The Magician's Nephew*:

> Polly had discovered long ago that if you opened a certain little door in the box-room attic of her house you would find the cistern and a dark place behind it which you could get into by a little careful climbing. The dark place was like a long tunnel with brick wall on one side and sloping roof on the other. In the roof there were little chinks of light between the slates. There was no floor in this tunnel: you had to step from rafter to rafter, and between them there was only plaster. If you stepped on this you would find yourself falling through the ceiling of the room below. Polly had used the bit of the tunnel just beside the cistern as a smugglers' cave. ... Here she kept a cash-box containing various treasures, and a story she was writing, and usually a few apples.[6]

That, I think, is a perfect description of what Jack's attic off the Little End Room must have been like for him as a boy.

BOXEN

What kind of stories did Jack write in the Little End Room? As I have already mentioned, Jack loved what he called "dressed animals," which he first discovered in the Beatrix Potter books. For his main characters, Jack combined this idea of dressed animals with knights in armor. Thus

---

6. *The Magician's Nephew*, chapter 1, pp. 7–8.

he wrote about valiant mice and rabbits riding out in full armor to kill, what else but cats, of course! From these stories Jack created a whole world which he called Animal Land.

Warnie, on the other hand, had different interests that led to his writing different sorts of stories. Jack's elder brother was a lover of India from a young age. And thus, so that they could create worlds and play more effectively together, Jack's Animal Land had to be related somehow to Warnie's India. The union of Warnie's India and Jack's Animal Land came to be known as the federation of Boxen.

Even in his childhood stories, Jack enjoyed setting his tales in the Middle Ages, hence the knights in shining armor. But to keep Warnie happy, Jack had to bring Animal Land into modern times, for Warnie had to have his trains and steamships. This led to Jack writing up the whole history of Animal Land from medieval to modern times. And then he made a map to show how Animal Land was placed in relationship to India.

You can already see, I am sure, that in making maps and writing the history of Animal Land, Jack was training himself to become a novelist. But it should also be clearly understood that the Animal Land of Jack's childhood was far different from the Narnia he created as a man of forty. Narnia has nothing in common with Animal Land except for dressed animals. Animal Land had no hint of wonder about it. One might say that Animal Land was all prose, whereas Narnia was more like poetry.

Writing stories of Boxen together was not to last for long. Soon enough, Warnie was sent off to a boarding school in England and thus removed from his brother for the better part of the year. It may sound rather cruel, but sending a ten-year-old off to boarding school in England was a typical thing to do for early twentieth-century Irish parents of some wealth, like Albert and Flora. Despite this separation, Jack stayed in touch with Warnie by letter, keeping his brother up-to-date on all the comings and goings of Boxen. On one occasion Jack wrote, "At present Boxen is *slightly* convulsed. The news has just reached her that King Bunny is a prisoner."[7]

---

7. Walter Hooper, editor, *The Collected Letters of C.S. Lewis*, Volume I, London: HarperCollins, 2000, p. 3.

Meanwhile, in real life at Little Lea, Jack continued to be home-schooled. He learned French and Latin from his mother and everything else from his governess, Annie Harper. Even with Warnie gone away to school, Jack had plenty of people with whom he could talk. He had his parents, of course. Then there was his Grandfather Lewis, who lived at Little Lea, though conversation was rather difficult with him since he was somewhat deaf. But there were also maids and a gardener as part of the household, as well as his governess, and Jack spoke with them all.

JOY

Even with so many people around him, young Jack preferred to be by himself most of the time. He began to live more and more in his own imaginary worlds. And some of Jack's imaginative happenings were the most important experiences of his young life. For example, there was the day when he stood by a flowering currant bush[8] and suddenly remembered the feeling of ecstasy when Warnie had brought his toy garden into the nursery.

Not only did some of young Jack's lively imaginative experiences come to him from Nature, but other overwhelming feelings were also stirred by reading certain books. Beatrix Potter's *Squirrel Nutkin* filled Jack with an unsatisfied desire for autumn, a season which remained his favorite for the rest of his life. Another experience of longing came to Jack while reading Longfellow's *Saga of King Olaf*. In the same book, Jack happened upon the unrhymed translation of "Tegner's Drapa":

I heard a voice, that cried,
"Balder the Beautiful
Is dead, is dead!"

---

8. You may think it silly, but I didn't realize what a currant bush was until I lived in Ireland with Douglas Gresham and had to pick currants. If you are as uninformed as I was then I should tell you: currants come in red and black varieties and they are delicious berries to eat, from which one can also make delectable juice and jelly.

Jack didn't know anything about Balder, but upon reading those lines he was filled with an almost sickening desire for the whole imaginary world of which Balder was a part. This was the same feeling that thrilled Jack's soul when he would glimpse the seemingly unending summer sunsets over the blue ridge of the Antrim Mountains north of Belfast.

This longing or desire Jack also called Joy. But it must be understood that Jack's Joy was far different from happiness or pleasure. Joy was a longing, an intense desire that was never completely satisfied. This experience was almost a kind of pain in Jack's soul, but it was a pain he wanted to experience over and over. The problem with Joy was that Jack couldn't simply call it up whenever he wanted to experience it again. Joy flitted across the screen of his imagination unasked for and oftentimes when he least expected it.

The Beginning of Winter

Even in the middle of summertime joy, the icy blasts of winter began to blow across young Jack's life. One night Jack had both a beastly headache and toothache at the same time. I think most people these days seldom have very bad toothaches, certainly compared to a hundred years ago, because our dental care is so much better now. If you do have a bit of a toothache, then hopefully, before you know it, your parents have packed you off to the dentist to have a filling. Such was not the case during Jack's childhood and so toothaches could be rather bad. What made Jack's toothache all the worse on this one night was that he was crying out for his mother to come and comfort him, but she could not come, because she was far more ill herself than Jack was. There were several doctors in Flora's bedroom; in those days doctors still made house calls and would often treat patients in their homes. Jack heard voices in the hall, and then his father coming into his room to relate the horrible news: Jack's mother Flora had cancer. An operation, also performed at Little Lea, soon followed. Jack prayed for his mother to be healed and Flora did, in fact, recover for a short while. Jack and his mother even traveled on another vacation together to the harbor city of Larne, north of Belfast.

As you might know, if you have ever had a family member suffering from cancer, part of the horror is that you lose the person you love long before they actually die. Your loved one may spend a lot of time in the hands of doctors, receiving various medical treatments. Towards the end, the person suffering from cancer may be taking so many pain-killing medicines that it is impossible for them to talk with you anymore. This is what Jack soon experienced. When Jack's prayers for healing no longer seemed to be working, he still hoped for a miracle, but it was not to be. When his prayers went seemingly unanswered, Jack thought no more of the "magician" God to whom he had prayed.

Warnie was hurriedly brought home from school in England. Flora, on her deathbed, presented Bibles to her two sons. Then, on August 23, 1908, her husband Albert's birthday, Flora Lewis died. Jack and Warnie were taken into their mother's bedroom to see her, or rather her body, lying there motionless, lifeless. Jack reacted to all the stuff of the funeral (the coffin, the hearse, the mourning clothes) much as any of us would at the age of nine: he hated it all.

Flora's death had two results for the Lewis family. First of all, Jack and Warnie were separated emotionally from their father. In the same year that Albert lost his wife, he lost his father and brother to "the grim reaper" as well. Understandably, Albert's grief was enormous and overwhelming. And his emotions, which had never been stable, became uncontrollable. There was a Shakespearean calendar hanging on the wall of the room where Flora died. The quotation on the page for the day of Flora's death read: "Men must endure their going hence." Albert preserved that calendar page for the rest of his life; he really never stopped grieving the loss of his beloved Flora.

The only way Albert's sons could handle his unpredictable emotions and his seemingly unjust behavior toward them was by pulling away. That was a bad result of Flora's passing. But there was a good result too—Jack and Warnie were drawn closer to each other. Still, all settled happiness was suddenly taken from Jack's life. He later said it was like the sinking of the island of Atlantis. The life he had known had disappeared and he was living in an entirely new world.

When Jack later wrote *The Magician's Nephew*, Digory's mother lay dying just like Jack's mother had. But Jack accomplished something in the story that he wasn't able to perform in real life. Digory brought home a magic apple from Aslan in Narnia to heal his mother. For Jack's own mother there was to be no such healing. Nine-year-old Jack just had to get on as best he could without her.

3

ALWAYS WINTER AND NEVER CHRISTMAS

"*The White Witch? Who is she?*"

"*Why, it is she that has got all Narnia under her thumb. It's she that makes it always winter. Always winter and never Christmas; think of that!*"[9]

This conversation between Lucy and Mr. Tumnus in *The Lion, the Witch and the Wardrobe* well describes the years of C.S. Lewis's life after his mother's death in 1908–"Always winter and never Christmas."

After the wintry blow of Flora's death, Albert packed Jack off to boarding school in England along with Warnie. Just one month after their mother's death, Jack and Warnie were taken by their father in a horse-drawn carriage to board a Fleetwood steam ship that would take them across the Irish Sea to England and a harsh new life. Jack hated the seemingly iron grip of the bowler hat, the horribly stiff Eton collar and the knickerbockers with the button at the knee which he was made to wear.

"Papy, why must I wear these terrible clothes?" asked Jack as the horse went clip-clop down the cobbled Belfast streets.

"It's all a necessary part of growing up," answered his father.

"But I don't want to be grown up! I want to wear shorts and sandals and play in the garden. Instead I feel as if I'm being sent to prison," Jack replied.

---

9. C.S. Lewis, *The Lion, the Witch and the Wardrobe*, New York: Macmillan, 1970, chapter 2, pp. 15–16.

Indeed, Jack later referred to his time at Wynyard School, Watford, Hertfordshire, north of London, as a "concentration camp" experience.

WYNYARD SCHOOL

What made the whole experience at Wynyard certifiably horrid was the fact that the headmaster of Jack's first school, Robert Capron, was quickly losing control of his mind, emotions and actions. At the drop of a hat, Mr. Capron would fly into a rage and show extreme cruelty toward some of the students in his charge. At first, Jack tried to make the best of a bad situation, even though he was deeply saddened by the loss of his mother and had been wrenched away from his home for the first time in his life at the tender age of nine years old. In his first letter home to his father from Wynyard, Jack even said, "I think I will be able to get on with Mr. Capron though to tell the truth he is rather eccentric." By Jack's second letter, written just ten days later, he was singing a different tune. Jack wrote to his father with a note of desperation: "Please may we not leave on Saturday? We simply *cannot* wait in this hole till the end of term."[10]

"What was so bad about Wynyard?" you may ask. Where shall I begin? When Jack arrived at the very dull-looking school building, which was really just a large house, Wynyard had only eight or nine boarders. There were also eight or nine day boys, that is, boys who attended daily but did not sleep at the school overnight. Organized games were eliminated from the school schedule shortly after Jack's arrival. Imagine your school without recess, with no playing outdoors, and you will begin to see the dismal picture of life at Wynyard. There was also no bathing, what we would call swimming, which was one of Jack's favorite activities throughout his life. And as to personal hygiene, each of the boarders was allowed only one bath per week. Oh, how life at Wynyard must have smelled!

---

10. *Collected Letters*, Volume I, pp. 6-7.

As far as the academic life at Wynyard School was concerned, there was hardly one to speak of. Jack had been capably doing Latin exercises under his mother's instruction before Wynyard, yet he was still doing only Latin exercises when he left Wynyard after two years. At a time when Jack would have loved beginning to read some classical authors in Latin, he was not given that privileged opportunity. Presumably, this was because the teaching at Wynyard was so poor.

In fact, Mr. Capron, or "Oldie" as he was called by the boarders behind his back, barely "taught" at all. Oldie's method consisted of calling his students to the front of the class one by one and asking them questions.

"Who was crowned king of the Grand Duchy of Lithuania on July 6, 1253?" Mr. Capron inquired of a boy named Rees.

"Lithuania, Mr. C?" Rees responded tentatively.

"Yes, Lithuania, Rees. Think, think, think!"

"I don't know anything about the Grand Duchy of Lithuania, Mr. C."

"Bring me my cane, Rees, I see I shall need it."

Oldie would often threaten students with a caning when their responses were wrong or incomplete. This punishment involved striking them across the back of the legs or the buttocks with a wooden cane. On many occasions Oldie followed through on his threat, though Jack miraculously escaped any physical punishment at Wynyard.

Much of the time Oldie did not even engage his students in discussion at all; he simply assigned them to do arithmetic sums. When the boys entered school at nine o'clock in the morning, they grabbed their chalk and slates and began doing sums. Occasionally they would be called forward to "say a lesson" as described above. When that was finished they would go back to doing sums. Jack later said of his time at Wynyard that all the other arts and sciences appeared as small islands in the midst of this vast ocean of arithmetic! At the end of every morning, each boy had to say how many sums he had done. Since there was little or no supervision of this work, Warnie had learned to tell his teacher that he had done five sums. No one ever asked *what* sums Warnie had done, so he did the same five sums every day!

"How did Albert end up sending his boys to such an awful school?" you may well wonder. Albert did not make a careless choice. His letters reveal that he considered many other schools before settling on Wynyard. However, one thing Albert did not do was to visit any of the schools in England which he was considering. Albert's search and selection were conducted entirely through the mail. And so, sight unseen, Albert unintentionally handed both of his sons into the care of a madman.

"But why," you might ask, "did Jack and Warnie not tell their father how bad the school really was?" The boys certainly made some attempts to tell their father that their school experience was not the best. By the late autumn of 1908, Albert was even thinking of taking his sons out of Wynyard. But after the first shock of this brutal environment wore off, Jack began to toughen up, no doubt helped by his brother Warnie. Neither Jack nor Warnie wanted their father to think that they were cowards. Besides, they had nothing with which to compare their school experience, presuming all such schools were equally loathsome. Thus, Jack gave up asking his father to remove him from the school.

And so Albert chose to leave Jack and Warnie at Wynyard School and some good did come of it. For the first few terms at Wynyard, Jack had Warnie's protection from any bullying. Soon enough, Jack made friends with the other boys at school and didn't have to rely on his brother so much.

In July 1909, Warnie was sent off by his father to Malvern College in Worcestershire, England. Malvern is what Americans would call a private preparatory school. A preparatory school prepares students for entrance to university. In fact, many Malvern students end up as students at Oxford University. We will learn more about that later.

By the summer of 1909, Jack had grown up somewhat. Though he was only ten years old, Jack was able to handle travel on his own from home in Ireland to school in England and back again. Jack and Warnie still traveled across the Irish Sea together, but then at Liverpool they would part company, Warnie going to Malvern and Jack to Wynyard.

As just mentioned, one good that came to Jack at Wynyard was the companionship of other boys around his own age. The grief Jack and Warnie experienced at home after their mother's death drew them closer to each other; in the same way, the suffering the boys at Wynyard experienced drew them together like a "band of brothers." And they *needed* to stick together. In time, Oldie's wife died and Oldie, overwhelmed by grief, became more violent than ever before.

In spite of the increasing unhappiness of life at Wynyard, it was there that Jack first attempted to practice his Christian faith. This came about through attendance at the worship services of St. John's Church in Watford. On one level, Jack reacted against these services because their style was very "high church"; that is to say, the services were much more like the Roman Catholic Church than what Jack was used to at home in Belfast. But it was at St. John's that Jack heard the main teachings of Christianity in a clear, unemotional manner for the first time. These services were not a particularly joyful experience; there was a great deal of fear stirred up in Jack's soul by the church. He lay awake on many a moonlit night in his curtainless dormitory fearing that his soul might end up in hell. However, the effect of this fear was entirely good: it led Jack to serious prayer, reading of the Bible and an attempt to obey his conscience.

Another good which came to Jack at Wynyard was that he learned to live by hope. At the beginning of each term it always seemed that the holidays and home were so far away. At times, it was just as hard for Jack to think of home as being real as it was for him to think of heaven as an actual place. And yet, gradually, over the course of the term, holiday and home took on an ever-increasing sense of reality. Soon enough, "this day next month" became "this day next week," and "this day next week" became "tomorrow." And then suddenly Jack was reunited with Warnie and they were on the ship home again crossing the Irish Sea. Jack later said that the life of Christian faith and the hope of heaven became more real to him because of his memories of life at school.

LIFE AT HOME

Meanwhile, what was life like for Jack and Warnie when they did return home on holiday? Every weekday from 9 o'clock in the morning until 6 o'clock in the evening, Jack and Warnie had the run of Little Lea because their father was at work. The only adults at home during those hours were the cook and the maid, and they were often arguing with each other so much that they took little or no notice of what Jack and Warnie were doing. This suited the Lewis boys to a T.

On one of those days Jack and Warnie decided it would be a wonderful thing to make a tent in the garden. They discovered a dust sheet in one of the attics of Little Lea which would serve as the perfect tarp. Next, all they needed was some wood for the tent poles. Warnie said to Jack, "We could make tent poles out of the stepladder in the wash house."

"By Jove, you're right, Warnie!" replied Jack excitedly.

In a matter of moments, the ladder was reduced to pieces as the boys took turns wielding a hatchet. The Lewis boys planted four of their "tent poles" in the ground and draped the dust sheet over the poles. It worked so well that Warnie was even able to sit atop the tent without it collapsing! Jack and Warnie, both being very courteous young men, realized they should put away their "tent" before their father returned from work. However, they forgot to put away the poles.

After dinner, when their father went for a walk with them in the garden, he noticed the pieces of the stepladder sticking out of the ground. Direct questioning soon followed. To their credit, Jack and Warnie told the truth on this occasion, but somehow that didn't make a difference to Albert. A flow of angry words came from their father's mouth. Albert's correction of his sons became overly dramatic. He started acting like he was trying a case in court. He finished by saying: "And what do I find but that you have cut up the stepladder. And for what? To make something like a failed puppet show!" At that moment, Jack and Warnie hid their faces from their father, not in fear, but to conceal their smiles. Suddenly their father's words seemed unbelievably funny to them and they wanted to burst into laughter. However, Jack and Warnie both knew better than to show their bemusement to Albert when he was in the heat of rage.

Since they were away at boarding school so many months out of every year, Jack and Warnie did not develop any close friendships with people their own age in Belfast. When they were home, Jack and Warnie preferred their own company. They liked reading, writing, playing, cycling and talking together better than the challenge of making friends outside of Little Lea. There was one major exception. Both of the Lewis brothers always enjoyed being invited to visit Glenmachan, the home of their mother's cousin, right around the corner from Little Lea. Glenmachan was the grandest house that Jack had ever encountered. Like most of the "big houses" of Ireland, Glenmachan was constructed of grey stone and had many chimneys, for of course, in the days of Jack's childhood, most rooms were heated by a fireplace.

Jack and Warnie especially enjoyed the well-wooded glen in which Glenmachan was situated. In some ways Glenmachan was simply a larger version of Little Lea, for there, too, Jack and Warnie enjoyed the attics, the indoor silences, and the seemingly endless bookshelves. But life at Glenmachan was more spacious and one had to be on one's best behavior when invited to a meal in the elegant Glenmachan dining room. The owners of Glenmachan were the wealthy Ewart family, who also owned one of the big linen-making companies for which Ireland is so renowned. In fact, their company at one time employed over 2500 workers, making it one of the largest companies of its kind in the western world.

After Flora Lewis died, Lady Ewart took upon herself the huge task of trying to civilize Jack and Warnie, who benefited much from her influence. Their relationship to the Ewart family also opened up many brand new experiences for them. It was through the Ewarts that Jack and Warnie first enjoyed the thrill of riding in an automobile. When Jack and Warnie were very young, the Ewart girls would give them carriage rides in a trap pulled by a stubborn donkey named Grisella. In later years, Jack and Warnie were entertained by members of the Ewart family at tennis parties. And invitations to lunch, picnics and the theater were showered on the Lewis brothers by the Ewarts.

One neighborhood event which Jack did not like at all, however, was dancing. Young people like Jack were invited to dancing parties by adults who wanted to teach them proper manners. To Jack, these events were sheer torment; he could never understand how a young man was supposed to enjoy dancing around on a polished floor late at night. Why should adults, to whom Jack had never done any harm, subject him to such torture? Dancing wasn't the only agony of these parties, for Jack soon discovered that one wasn't supposed to talk about anything really interesting at these events. When Jack did speak the only language he knew, that of his beloved books, others simply laughed at him. So Jack learned to speak the only language allowed at such parties—small talk. This was largely polite conversation—about the weather, the surroundings, cultural events and other dull topics—which Jack would despise for the rest of his life.

CAMPBELL COLLEGE

In the spring of 1910, Jack's "concentration camp" experience at Wynyard School came to a close. Robert Capron wrote to Albert Lewis to tell him that he was giving up schoolwork and that therefore another school would need to be found for Jack. Oldie gave up being headmaster to become the pastor of a church, but that did not last long either. He began beating the choirboys and eventually ended up in a mental hospital where he died in 1911.

Jack was thrilled to be free of Oldie and of Wynyard School. On top of that delight, his father came up with a plan which pleased Jack no end. He was to attend Campbell College, a boys' preparatory school only a mile away from Little Lea. Jack entered the red brick walls and towers of Campbell as a boarder, but he was allowed to come home every Sunday. Campbell was like English prep schools Jack would later become familiar with in that it had prefects, boys who were the leaders of certain houses. Otherwise, Campbell was not like an English school at all, for there was no rigid social ladder. What bullying went on at Campbell was of a more democratic variety.

Only once did this bullying come Jack's way; the story of it is interesting enough to be worthy of the telling. One day, while Jack was minding his own business, he was suddenly dragged at a ferocious speed through the long corridors of Campbell by a gang of resident hoodlums. When Jack was finally able to get his bearings, he found himself with several other "prisoners" in a bare, half-lit room. The first "guinea pig" was lifted to his feet by the "gangsters" and made to bend over, obviously in preparation for a good spanking. But rather than spanking their victim, two of the bullies gave the first prisoner a good shove and he suddenly disappeared. After the same routine was followed with several other victims disappearing without a sound and without a trace, it was Jack's turn. He, too, received a good shove from behind and immediately found himself hurtling through a chute into what turned out to be a coal cellar. Another boy came zooming in behind Jack; then their captors shut and bolted the coal chute with a whoop and a holler as they went off to capture more victims. Eventually, Jack and the other prisoners were set free, black with soot, but otherwise none the worse for wear.

One might wonder if Jack learned anything more at Campbell than he had at Wynyard. The answer is: a little bit. For it was at Campbell that Jack had one of his first great encounters with English poetry; this was in the form of the poem "Sohrab and Rustum" by Matthew Arnold. From the moment that Jack first read the poem, he fell in love with what he called the "silvery coolness," the very atmosphere created by Arnold's words. This poem prepared Jack to like the work of the Greek writer, Homer, when he met it later on in his schooling.

However, halfway through his first and only term at Campbell, Jack became ill and was sent on the one-mile journey home to Little Lea. From the time that Jack was very young, it was thought that he had a weak chest. And so Albert decided to remove Jack from Campbell permanently and send him to a location that might be better for his health. Albert landed on the idea of sending Jack to Great Malvern in England. This was a Victorian spa town where many people of an earlier generation would travel on holiday to drink the healing waters of the Malvern springs. Albert had learned of a good preparatory school called Cherbourg, in the same town, to which he decided to send Jack. And most conveniently, Warnie was in attendance at nearby Malvern College, allowing him to look out for his younger brother.

The six weeks Jack had home alone with his father before the Christmas holiday and departure for England with Warnie were a complete delight. Jack and Albert were "famously snug together" and got along well without Warnie there to drag Jack into mischief. While his father was at work, Jack reveled in the opportunity to read, write and draw to his heart's content. It was at this time that Jack fell under the spell of fairy tales, especially tales with dwarfs in them. Jack's imagination was so filled with these little earthmen that one day while walking in his own garden at Little Lea Jack thought he saw a dwarf run past him into the bushes!

This was Jack's first encounter with such little people, but it wouldn't be his last. It is no wonder, given Jack's early interest in leprechauns and all the rest, that he would have an important role for dwarfs when he came to write *The Chronicles of Narnia* many years later.

4

Looking for an Escape

Considering how awful Jack's early experiences in boarding school were, I am sure he often wished he could escape into some magical land through the door of his grandfather's wardrobe at Little Lea. This tall, dark, intricately carved wooden wardrobe may have served as part of the inspiration for *The Lion, the Witch and the Wardrobe*. When Douglas Gresham first met Jack many years later and saw this old wardrobe for the first time, he asked Jack, "Is this the wardrobe from the story?"

Jack responded, "It might be!"

However, at the age of twelve, Jack had no glimmers of Narnia. He had only the sense of anxiety that any young person would feel when they have a new school to face.

Cherbourg School

In January 1911, Jack set out with Warnie across the Irish Sea once again. This time they were en route together to Great Malvern, England, just across the border from Wales. The brothers' favorite part of the trip was stopping over in Liverpool. Jack and Warnie quickly learned that they could spend the whole morning in the Lime Street Hotel and catch the late train for Malvern. That way they could have more fun and arrive at the latest allowable time at their different schools. The brothers would spend their morning in the hotel lounge, smoking cigarettes and reading magazines and books. (Yes, both the Lewis boys started smoking, without their father's immediate knowledge, at a very young age. Of course, this was a very bad thing to do. However, at the beginning of the twentieth century no one knew how bad smoking was for one's health.)

The return journey through Liverpool was even more fun for the boys. First, there was dinner at a restaurant. Then they would visit the old Empire, a music hall in the city where some of the great vaudeville shows were performed. After the show, Jack and Warnie would make their way to the Liverpool docks where they would board their ship. Soon they would hear the ship's fog horn blast and taste the spray of sea salt on their lips as England receded behind them into the night.

Jack's first sight of Great Malvern changed his entire opinion of England. He had disliked the flat and flinty landscape of Watford, Hertfordshire, surrounding Wynyard School. (Since Jack's time, the town has been smothered by the sprawling growth of Greater London.) Malvern was completely different. The town itself hugged the rugged cliffs of the Malvern Hills where the air was fresh and clean. On a clear day, from the British Camp, the remains of an Iron Age fort atop those hills, one could see far into wild Wales on one side of the mountain range and into the rich farmland of the Cotswolds on the other. Malvern was also possessed of the first beautiful building Jack ever saw—Malvern Priory. The Priory Church has a great central Norman tower and some of the finest medieval stained glass windows in all of England, as well as medieval tiles and beautifully carved wooden seats in the choir stalls.

Though Jack was entranced by the beauty of Malvern Priory, it was in Malvern that Jack temporarily lost his Christian faith. Jack ceased to be a Christian while he was living as a boarder at Cherbourg School, a tall, white building further up in the Malvern Hills overlooking the College. The first contributing factor to Jack's loss of faith was his matron, Miss Cowie. The matron was responsible for caring for the schoolboys in her charge, sort of like a mother hen. All the boys loved Miss C, especially Jack, since he had lost his own mother three years before. However, Miss C contributed unknowingly to Jack's loss of Christian conviction. Miss C was not a Christian herself; she was wandering in the mazes of what we today would call "New Age" thinking. Miss C believed in all sorts of spirits, the kind of thing Jack had thought was only fairy tale stuff up to that point in time. Suddenly, young Jack realized that Christianity was not the only religion "on the market." There really were people who believed things vastly different from the religion of his father and extended family back home in Belfast.

The reason this startled Jack so much was that he already had a secret desire to be done with Christianity anyway. This was due to a very wrong notion Jack had gotten into his head years before. As a child, he had been taught that one should not only say one's prayers but also really think about what one was saying. And so if he prayed the Lord's Prayer and didn't think he *felt* the words properly, then he would start all over again. You can imagine that this led to many sleepless nights for Jack as he worried about whether he was getting his bedtime prayers just right.

Another thing which led Jack to abandon the faith of his childhood was his reading of classic literature, especially the Latin author, Virgil. In Virgil, Jack was presented with a multitude of religious ideas. Neither Jack's teachers nor the editors of the books Jack was reading took the time to explain why certain religious ideas were wrong and the Christian ones were right. So Jack came to the conclusion that all religion was a bunch of nonsense into which humans blundered from time to time. I remember having the same doubts when I first read Greek mythology in middle school. "How do we know that there is only one God who has revealed himself in Jesus Christ?" I wondered. "Why not believe in a pantheon of gods as the Greeks did?"

There was also a third thing which influenced Jack's loss of Christian faith. Even before his mother's death, Jack was beginning to have the feeling that everything in the universe would do precisely what you didn't want it to do. This feeling was first formed in Jack because of his inability to make anything with his hands due to the missing joint in his thumbs.

And then when Jack's mother died in spite of his desperate prayers for her healing, Jack's conclusion was sealed; he was convinced that he was living in an evil universe. His whole outlook was further shaped by his horrible experiences in school and his father's stifling work life. Jack figured there wasn't much to life other than school terms followed by holidays followed by more school terms and then work, work, work until you die.

A final influence which led Jack to become an atheist was the reading that he did for fun. H. G. Wells was one of Jack's favorite authors at the time, and Wells' books firmly put in his mind the idea that the universe was a vast and cold place of mostly empty space; according to Wells, human beings were something less than ants in comparison to the seemingly never-ending universe. Jack came to the conclusion that if a good god had designed the world, it would not be such a bad world. And so, gradually, with what he felt to be a great sense of relief, Jack simply let the Christian faith of his childhood slip away. There was no more summertime Joy for a while; the landscape of Jack's imagination now had nothing but a bleak wintry backdrop.

The Return of Joy

While it would be some time before Jack would rediscover the truths of the Christian faith, his imaginative deep-freeze was not to last for long. Soon there was a fresh wind of springtime Joy blowing. The source of the new breeze was a literary magazine, the December 1911 issue of *The Bookman*, which someone had left open in one of the classrooms at Cherbourg. On the open page Jack spied a headline and a picture. The words which struck the chord of longing once again in Jack's soul were these: *Siegfried and the Twilight of the Gods*. The picture was one of Arthur Rackham's illustrations of the first part of composer Richard Wagner's *Ring Cycle*. Jack knew nothing before that moment about the character of Siegfried or the composer Wagner. But suddenly a vision of the endless twilight of Northern summer filled his imagination. Jack knew that he was experiencing, once again, the same feeling he had had upon reading those lines from "Tegner's Drapa" about Balder. Jack knew that he was recovering the Joy which he had not experienced since before his mother had died. But just as soon as he knew what he was feeling, the sensation left him and Jack longed to experience the Joy all over again.

In order to recover the Joy, Jack tried to learn all he could about Wagner and his opera, *The Ring*. He even wrote his own heroic poem about the Nibelung story; Jack's composition, *Loki Bound*, was Norse in subject but Greek in form. Eventually Jack's ears thrilled to hear a recording of *The Ride of the Valkyries* and he sought to learn all he could about Norse mythology. With the return of Joy, Jack began to live two lives—an inner one of the imagination and an outer one of school, exams, companionship with fellow students, and trips home for the holidays.

The most important event in Jack's outer life at this time took place in June 1913. He sat for a scholarship examination for entrance to Malvern College. Unfortunately, Jack fell ill on the first of June but still had to take the exams. He had tests in Latin and Greek grammar, Latin prose, English, a general paper in History and Geography, Scripture, French, Arithmetic and Algebra. Amazingly, Jack passed his exams and won the scholarship despite being ill with a high fever!

MALVERN COLLEGE

In September 1913, Jack went to Malvern College while Warnie went to live with a tutor and his wife in Surrey, England. The tutor, William T. Kirkpatrick, would prep Warnie for entrance to Sandhurst Military Academy. Going to Malvern College was the most exciting thing that had happened in Jack's outer life to date. Based upon Warnie's reports of the college, Jack was ready to humbly submit to the Bloods, the adored athletes and prefects of the school.

Jack's first hours at the college, with its expansive green playing fields and commanding view of Malvern, were memorable. He was to be a member of the oldest dormitory, School House, just like Warnie before him.

School House was Victorian Gothic in style—a tall, narrow building of brownish stone similar to the other main buildings on campus. The floor of School House on which Jack lived consisted of two stone corridors at right angles to one another. Off of these halls were the individual studies, each six feet square, and each belonging to two or three boys. Each study was crammed full of bookcases, cupboards, knick-knacks and pictures. It all seemed luxurious to Jack after the very simple life of Wynyard, Campbell and Cherbourg.

Jack's first days were spent quickly trying to figure out what he was supposed to do and how to get around where he needed to go. First of all, he had to discover which Club he was in. Clubs were the groups that boys were assigned to for the purpose of required sports. Jack had to find the notice board where Clubs were posted. Unfortunately, Jack was forced away from the board by the crowd of other boys before he had time to read it. He was also under a time crunch to get to his next assigned activity.

When he got back to School House an older boy, one of the Bloods, said to Jack, "You're in my club, Lewis. B6."

"Thanks very much," responded Jack.

From then on, Jack went to the B6 notice board to see where he was supposed to play and when. Thankfully, his name was never on the board! Jack was not good at sports and so he looked at games as only a necessary evil of life. Jack put sports in the same category as paying income tax or going to the dentist.

In the end, Jack found out that the School House Blood had lied to him; he wasn't in B6 Club at all. In fact, Jack was in serious trouble for skipping out on games. Worse still, his punishment was to be given not by an adult faculty member at the school, but by a senior student, the "Head" of the college. In the end, the punishment Jack received from the Head wasn't all that bad. But now Jack was a marked man, he was known as one who "skipped Clubs" and so the Bloods of School House were always on the lookout for other mistakes Jack might make.

One of the worst parts of life at the college for Jack was the fact that the new boys had to serve the older boys. When a Blood wanted his army training kit brushed, or his boots cleaned, or his study set in order, or his tea prepared, he would call for one of the new boys in the labor pool. Jack dreaded hearing the call, "Oh, young Lewis, I've got a job for you!"

Though he had won a scholarship to Malvern, Jack could barely keep up with the amount of advanced schoolwork he had to do. And now on top of that, he had to do the work of a slave for any Blood who called on him. By the end of each day, Jack was dog-tired, and for more than one reason. Jack was at that stage of physical growth where he had temporarily outgrown his own strength, so games wore him out. He was also having trouble with his teeth and so was in real pain a lot of the time. Furthermore, Jack grew mentally and emotionally tired from having to pretend he was interested in the things Bloods thought were important—like sports. Even for those who were athletically talented, games were no fun at Malvern College because the competition was too fierce. For all these reasons and more, Jack came to hate the place he had been so prepared to love.

There were two exceptions to this hatred. One was Jack's teacher, Harry Wakelyn Smith, or "Smewgy," as he was called by some of his students. As a teacher and a human being, Jack rated Smewgy "beyond expectation, beyond hope." Apparently others gave Mr. Smith high marks as well, for when I visited Malvern College in 1997 his portrait hung in his old classroom above a memorial dedicated to him.

Smewgy had gray hair by the time Jack knew him and wore very large glasses. He had a wide mouth which gave him a froglike expression, but according to Jack there was nothing frog-like about his voice. The man was "honey-tongued" and so every bit of poetry he read turned into music.

Smewgy was a man of perfect courtesy, something so lacking in our day that I had better describe it for you. Smewgy always addressed the boys in his schoolroom as "gentlemen," and so the possibility of acting in any other manner was ruled out from the first day of class. For example, on one very hot day, which happens only rarely in England, Smewgy said, "Gentlemen, you may remove your coats in class today."

Then Smewgy said, "And may I have your permission to remove my gown?" All college and university teachers in England wore black gowns during instruction in those days.

In short, to be taught by Harry Wakelyn Smith was to have one's life ennobled. As you will soon see, Jack modeled his own teaching manner very much on that of his favorite teacher.

The other exception to Jack's dislike of Malvern College was "the Gurney," which was the name of the college library. Jack loved the Gurney not only because of the books but because it was an oasis for him in the midst of the desert of games and constantly having to slave for the Bloods. Once Jack was inside the Gurney, he was a free man. To be sure, he had to "run the gauntlet" to get there. Any number of things or people might prevent him from spending his free time in the library. Jack might be put down for Clubs or he might have to attend a school cricket match and cheer for the Malvern team. While he was on his way to the Gurney he might be stopped in his tracks by a Blood and ordered to perform some menial task. However, once Jack was inside the library, the quiet and the leisure created a space where those few moments were made eternal. It was in the Gurney that Jack discovered the works of John Milton, William Butler Yeats and a book on Celtic mythology to add to his already beloved Norse myths.

Despite these two great blessings at Malvern, Jack never gave up asking his father for permission to leave the school. And then suddenly, in the summer of 1914, Jack got his wish; his father provided the escape from school Jack had been longing for.

What had happened was this: William Kirkpatrick had done an excellent job prepping Warnie for entrance to Sandhurst. So Albert Lewis thought perhaps Kirkpatrick, or "the Great Knock," as the Lewises called him, might do an even better job prepping Jack for the entrance exam to Oxford University. Jack was overjoyed at the prospect. Simply the thought of never having to play sports again was enough to make Jack bust his buttons. Imagine how you would feel if it was suddenly announced that there were to be no more exams—in fact, no more grading at all in school—and you will have some idea of how Jack felt about going to live with a "crammer" in Surrey.

At the same time that Albert decided to send Jack to Kirkpatrick for tutoring, another great blessing was poured into Jack's lap. I mentioned earlier how Jack and Warnie never made friends at home in Belfast because they were away so many months of the year. While that was a true statement, it would *not* be true to say that no one in the neighborhood of Little Lea ever tried to make friends with the Lewis boys. There was one boy who lived almost directly across the street from Little Lea whose name was Arthur Greeves. Arthur was the same age as Warnie, but he tried repeatedly to make friends with Jack. Arthur had even been a student at Campbell College, but he and Jack never crossed paths there.

At any rate, shortly before Jack's final term at Malvern, he was home on holiday and one day received a message from the Greeves' residence. The message was that Arthur was ill in bed and would appreciate a visit from Jack. For some unexplainable reason, Jack accepted this invitation despite the fact that he had repeatedly snubbed Arthur in the past. When Jack called on Arthur, he found him sitting up in bed with a copy of *Myths of the Norsemen* on his bedside table.

"Do *you* like that?" asked Jack.

"Do *you* like that?" asked Arthur.

In the next moment their two heads were together poring over the book. Very quickly these two teenagers discovered that not only did they both like the same book, but they liked it for the same reason. Both had experienced Joy, a joy that came from their immersion in Norse mythology.

After the wintry blast of his mother's death, Jack probably wondered if he would ever know happiness again. But by 1914, the icy winter of Jack's life was beginning to thaw just as the White Witch's winter did in Narnia once Aslan was on the move. In the next chapter, we will begin to discover just how much Aslan was on the move in young Jack's life.

THE CALLING
OF A HEATHEN

Anne Jenkins from Hertfordshire, England, was ten years old when she wrote to C.S. Lewis to ask him a question about something in *The Silver Chair*, the fourth Narnia book to be published. Toward the end of the book, as I am sure you will remember, Caspian is brought back to life by Aslan. Anne wondered what Lewis meant in that chapter when he wrote that "most people have died."

In response to Anne's letter, Lewis wrote back giving a very full description of the Christian meaning behind the Narnia stories:

> *The whole Narnian story is about Christ. That is to say, I asked myself 'Supposing that there really was a world like Narnia and supposing it had (like our world) gone wrong and supposing Christ wanted to go into that world and save it (as He did ours) what might have happened?' The stories are my answers.* [11]

Regarding *The Horse and His Boy*, the fifth Narnia book published, but the third book in the chronology of Narnia, Lewis said the story was about "the calling and conversion of a heathen." The word "heathen" is not used much anymore but it means, very simply, a person who does not believe in the God of the Bible. The heathen Jack was talking about was Shasta, who

---

11. Walter Hooper, *C.S. Lewis: Companion & Guide*, New York: HarperCollins, 1996, p. 426.

lived in Calormen for most of his young life and did not know the great lion Aslan of Narnia.

From 1914 to 1917, Jack was very much like the young Shasta, a teenager wandering through life without any personal knowledge of, or hope in, the one true God. Though Jack Lewis would not begin a personal relationship with Jesus Christ until 1931, we will see in this chapter that there were many ways in which God began to call out to him and make his presence known.

The Great Knock

This new chapter in Jack's life began with him traveling to Great Bookham, Surrey, England, to be tutored by William Kirkpatrick. Kirkpatrick had been Albert's teacher and headmaster at Lurgan College, County Armagh, Ireland when Albert was a schoolboy. It was at Lurgan that Kirkpatrick had received the nickname, "The Great Knock." Kirkpatrick retired in 1899 and had moved to the somewhat warmer climate of Surrey, southwest of London.

Great Bookham is a lovely little village filled with winding narrow lanes, red brick and half-timbered buildings with red tile roofs. Gastons, the house in which the Old Knock lived with his wife, is no longer in existence, and that is too bad, because it was in that house that Jack spent many of the happiest days of his life.

Jack arrived at Bookham Station on a September day in 1914, apprehensive about his first meeting with Kirkpatrick. Albert had described Kirkpatrick as an emotional sort of character. According to Albert, on one occasion when Albert was a schoolboy and had gotten into some sort of difficulty, Kirkpatrick was the picture of compassion. As the story goes, the Old Knock drew Albert aside, very naturally put his arm around the boy, rubbed his whiskers gently against Albert's smooth cheek and whispered some words of comfort.

Ever since his mother's death, Jack had been very wary of emotions in general so he looked forward to this first meeting with the "soft" old tutor about as much as you or I would look forward to a firing squad. But there was nothing to be done about it; when Jack got off the train at Bookham, there was the old softy himself. Jack wondered if Kirkpatrick would hug him right away or wait until later. The first sight of Kirkpatrick's long side-burns alarmed Jack to no end. However, the six-foot-tall, shabbily dressed, thin man with his wrinkled and muscular face, smelling of pipe tobacco, greeted Jack with only a vice-grip handshake.

As they walked away from the station, the Great Knock said, "We are now traveling along the main artery between Great and Little Bookham."

In response, Jack thought he was expected to make small talk as he had learned to do at the dancing parties in Belfast. So Jack told the Old Knock, "The scenery of Surrey is much wilder than I had expected."

Immediately Kirk shouted, "Stop!" and asked Jack, "What do you mean by 'wildness' and what grounds did you have for not expecting it?"

Jack proceeded to make more small talk and Kirk continued to pull apart and analyze everything Jack was saying. Finally, Jack realized that the Old Knock was really interested in what he had to say! Kirk asked, "Upon what have you based your opinion of Surrey, Mr. Lewis?"

Up to that point in time, Jack never realized his opinions needed to be based on anything. The Old Knock concluded, "Therefore, Mr. Lewis, you have no right to have any opinion about Surrey whatsoever since your opinion is not based on any accurate knowledge!"

Far from being a very emotional person, Jack quickly discovered that Kirkpatrick was the most logical person he had ever met.[12] Some young men would not have enjoyed this constant examination of communication, but to Jack's hungry mind, starving to learn, daily conversation with Kirk was like sitting down to a feast. Here was a man who was not so much in-terested in *you* as in what you *said*, and that suited Jack perfectly.

There was only one part of Kirkpatrick's life that was not logical at all. The man had been brought up as an Ulster Scot Presbyterian but had long since given up the faith and become an atheist. Yet, every Sunday when he

---

12. As you may have guessed, C.S. Lewis based the character of Professor Kirke in the Narnia books partly on William Kirkpatrick and partly on himself.

worked in his garden, he would wear a slightly finer suit of clothes than he would to perform the same job on a weekday. Though Kirk said he no longer believed in God, he somehow still couldn't be persuaded to give up some of the Sabbath-keeping habits of his boyhood.

Jack arrived at Gastons on a Saturday and began translating the work of the Greek poet, Homer, on Monday. The first thing after breakfast on Monday morning, the Great Knock sat down next to Jack in the study and began reading from the *Iliad*, Book I, in Greek. Even while reading aloud in an ancient and foreign language, Kirk's Northern Irish (Ulster) accent with the rolling of his R's still came through. Kirk then translated for Jack about a hundred lines of the Greek poetry he had just read. After that he handed Jack a Greek-English dictionary and asked Jack to write down his own translation of as much of Homer as he could get through. At first, Jack could not get very far at all, but eventually he ended up being able to think in Greek. Many years later, after Jack returned to the Christian faith, he would read the New Testament in Greek every day.

What else did Jack study with the Old Knock? It might be better to ask: What didn't he study? Jack read all of the classical Greek and Roman authors in their original languages. And in the evening Jack learned French from Mrs. Kirkpatrick who taught that language in a similar manner to the way her husband taught Greek. Soon Jack was reading some of the great French novels on his own. For the first couple of weeks, the Old Knock gave Jack direction for his reading in English literature. However, Kirk soon discovered that Jack needed no guidance in this subject; Jack always made a beeline for the best authors, just as most teenagers would quickly find the best pizza parlor in town. However, Homer came first in Jack's studies. After reading and translating the *Iliad*, Kirk and Jack moved on to the entire *Odyssey*.

What did Jack do in his free time? On the weekends he loved hiking through the countryside of Surrey. And during the two years he was at Gastons, Jack wrote one letter per week to his father, because he had to, and one letter to his friend Arthur Greeves, because he wanted to. Jack's weekly letters to Arthur from this time period tell us much about Jack's life and his vast reading, among other things.

Though Jack and Arthur shared a love of books, they were very different in other ways. Arthur was the youngest member of a large family, yet Arthur's home was usually quieter than Jack's for some reason. Arthur's family members were part of the Plymouth Brethren Church, whereas Jack's father was a tried and true Anglican. Arthur, rather than going to university like Jack soon would, was working in the business belonging to one of his brothers. Where Jack had become a healthy and hearty young man, Arthur's health was more delicate. This led to Arthur eventually giving up work altogether and living off of his family's great wealth. Jack was mainly a person of one talent: writing. Arthur had a number of talents: piano, music composition and painting. In fact, I have seen one of Arthur's paintings, of a barley field at harvest time, in the home of C.S. Lewis's stepson, Douglas Gresham.

Despite their differences, or maybe because of them, Arthur and Jack were able to learn much from one another. Arthur taught Jack to enjoy some of the great British novelists like Sir Walter Scott and Jane Austen. Arthur also taught Jack to have a love for what he called "homeliness." By the word "homely," Jack and Arthur both meant the sheer goodness of simple things like weather (sun, rain, fog, snow and even flat, grey days), food, family and the countryside. These two teenage friends deeply enjoyed walking or hiking together when Jack was at home in Belfast. I'm sure they talked about everything under the sun as they went along together, breathing deep of the fresh country air with the smell of heather in the wind.

By contrast, just as his friendship with Arthur was blossoming, Jack's relationship with his father Albert was getting worse and worse. Every holiday, Jack would return home with a little more education under his belt and more clarity to his thought and speech. The more Jack developed his own brainpower, the more muddle-headed he thought his own father was. Unfortunately, Jack allowed himself to become irritated with traits in his father which he would later find to be delightful quirks in other old men.

However, much of the problem between father and son stemmed from the fact that Albert would hardly give Jack any breathing room when he was at home. For example, one day Jack received a letter from Warnie and Albert immediately demanded to see it. Albert, upon reading the letter, said, "Your brother has made some comments about this mutual acquaintance of yours which are completely unfair!"

In Warnie's defense, Jack reminded his father, "The letter was not addressed to you, Papy."

Albert simply could not understand that. He insisted, "Warnie must have known I would see the letter. I'm sure Warnie *wanted* me to read it!" Albert could not imagine that his sons would want to keep anything secret from him.

This poor relationship between father and son helps to explain something dishonest Jack did at this time. While home on holiday, he allowed himself to be prepared for confirmation at St. Mark's Dundela. Jack was actually confirmed and took his first Communion, all the while knowing that he was not a believer in the teachings of Christianity. Jack did this because he simply could not bring himself to confess to his father that he had become an atheist. Jack feared that his father could never be made to understand his reasons for abandoning the faith and so Jack simply told him nothing; Jack allowed his father to go on thinking that he was still a believer when he most certainly was not.

In his letters to Arthur, Jack was much more honest about his true thoughts and feelings. In the autumn of 1916, Jack wrote to Arthur saying, "You ask me my religious views: you know, I think, that I believe in no religion. There is absolutely no proof for any of them and, from a philosophical standpoint, Christianity is not even the best."[13]

Despite Jack's professed atheism, a very important event took place during his time at Great Bookham. This event began to move him, without his own conscious knowledge, back toward Christian faith. One day in 1916, Jack wrote to Arthur to tell him he had a great literary experience that week. What had happened was this: Jack was in the habit of taking a walk from Great Bookham to the nearby town of Leatherhead every week. And then he would take the train back to Bookham. On this particular excursion, Jack spied a book in the station bookshop which he thought he might

---

13. *Collected Letters*, Vol. I, p. 230.

like to read. So he bought it. The book was George MacDonald's *Phantastes*. Jack began reading the book that evening. *Phantastes* is the story of Anodos, a young man who is pulled into a dreamlike world where he hunts for his ideal of female beauty. Anodos lives through many adventures and temptations while in the other world, until he is finally ready to give up his ideals. Jack later said that reading this fairy tale baptized his imagination; specifically, reading *Phantastes* filled Jack's mind with an atmosphere of holiness. What Jack didn't know was that God was calling to him through the writing of a committed Christian, George MacDonald.

Up to Oxford

Jack's perfect time with the Great Knock was soon coming to an end. In December 1916, Jack went up to Oxford from Great Bookham to take a scholarship examination for entrance to one of the colleges of Oxford University. Unfortunately, after he got off the train in Oxford, Jack took a wrong turn out of the railway station. Unknowingly, he was walking away from the center of the great city itself. Jack was confused. Could all of these ugly storefronts really be part of the glorious university town he had heard of most of his life? Only when the storefronts came to an end and Jack reached open fields did he turn around and look. What he saw in the distance were the "dreaming spires" of the university, the spectacular skyline of Oxford's medieval architecture. Late in the day from this viewpoint, Jack would have seen the dome of Radcliffe Camera, the spire of St. Mary's Church and all the other college buildings, their mellow Cotswold stone glowing golden at sunset. Jack later thought of this little incident as an allegory of his whole life. He would spend much of his time from 1917 until 1929 walking away from the center of Christianity. However, when he finally turned around to look at what he had left behind, he caught a glimpse of Christ in all his glory.

On Jack's first full day in Oxford, snow began to fall, turning all the spires of all the churches and the pinnacles on all the colleges into what looked like glistening white wedding cake decorations. Jack had never seen anything as beautiful as Oxford, especially as he walked among its enchanting buildings on the frosty moonlit nights of his first visit.

The tests that Jack had to take to be accepted as a student at Oxford were given in Oriel College, one of the now thirty-nine colleges which belong to Oxford University and famed for its rowing tradition. The scholarship examinations took place from December 5 to 9 in Oriel's dining hall underneath its dark brown hammer-beam ceiling with the winter sunlight shining through the glowing stained glass windows. On the first day of testing, the weather was freezing. And English buildings in 1916 did not have very good heating systems. Jack and the other students wore heavy winter clothing while sitting inside Oriel College to take their tests. They even tried to write with their gloves on; it was that cold!

Jack had to take exams in Latin, Greek and English. But he got a huge break with the first essay he was assigned; it was all about one of his favorite authors, Samuel Johnson. And even some of the Latin and Greek translations Jack had to write were translations from texts Jack had studied with the Great Knock. Still, Jack didn't have much self-confidence; after the test was over he told his father that he had almost certainly failed.

As things turned out, Jack didn't need to worry. Almost on Christmas Eve, back home in Belfast, he received a letter from the Master of University College, Oxford, Reginald W. Macan. The letter announced that University College (hereafter referred to as "Univ") had elected Jack to a scholarship. The Master's letter further asked what Jack's plans were until the following October. Jack wasn't sure what his plans would be so he asked Macan how he should spend the next few months of his life. The Master told him that all the students at Univ were enrolled in military service, except for those who were physically disabled in some way.

It was at this point that Jack made a very important decision. He decided to enlist in the army and fight for England during The Great War, what we now call World War I. As an Irish citizen, Jack didn't have to serve in the army. But he felt a sense of duty to the country where he would be living as a student. And so he made the commitment and followed through on it.

6

Narnia and the North!

The continual cry throughout *The Horse and His Boy* is "for Narnia and the North." In a sense, the third Narnian chronicle is all about Shasta's journey from Calormen in the south to Narnia in the north; it is a journey for Shasta from slavery to freedom. At the age of eighteen, Jack was about to embark on a new stage of his own life journey—from Great Bookham in the south of England to Oxford, a bit further north in the heart of England. Jack didn't know it, but in 1917, he was also beginning a journey from spiritual slavery to spiritual freedom.

Getting Into Oxford

The Great Knock was still not out of Jack's life. Kirkpatrick wrote to Albert in January 1917, suggesting that Jack should take Responsions, the Oxford University entrance examinations. Even though Jack had been admitted to University College he would not, according to the unusual Oxford system, be a student of the university as a whole unless he passed Responsions. Kirkpatrick thought it best to get these entrance examinations out of the way, even if Jack was going to serve in the army. The Old Knock even offered to help Jack prepare for Responsions, especially the mathematics portion, which was not Jack's strongest subject.

Jack left Belfast at the end of January and stopped over in Oxford to have a talk with the Master of University College. The Master promised that if Jack passed Responsions, to be given in March, he could come up to Oxford at the beginning of Trinity Term[14] and join the Officer Training Corps in preparation for entrance to army life. So Jack went from Oxford to Great Bookham to have Kirkpatrick prep him for Responsions.

During Jack's time with Kirkpatrick in early 1917, he took up the study of Italian (to add to his French and German) in case he should *not* gain entrance to Oxford. Having Italian, French and German under his belt might help him get a job working for the British government in their foreign service, if nothing else. In early February, Jack read the first two hundred lines of Dante's *Divine Comedy*, in Italian, with much success. Jack continued his vast reading in all of these languages, as well as Latin and English, during this time. His reading included no less than twenty-one of the great authors of the western tradition.

As much as Jack enjoyed living again with the Old Knock and his wife and reading to his heart's content, that pleasant time all too quickly came to an end. Jack took Responsions starting on March 20 and he returned to Belfast before the end of the month. Soon thereafter, he learned that he had failed the algebra portion of the exam. However, he was allowed to start living at Univ during Trinity Term in order to enter the army through the University Officers' Training Corps (OTC).

Jack arrived back in Oxford at the end of April and officially became a member of University College. He was supposed to prepare for a second try at Responsions to be taken again the following term, and so began algebra lessons with a faculty member at Hertford College, Oxford. On April 30, Jack joined the OTC and had a physical exam with a doctor. He weighed 182 pounds and measured 5 feet 10 ¾ inches tall. The commanding officer of the OTC told Jack: "You may make a useful officer but you won't have enough training to enter the Officer Cadet Unit until the end of June."

---

14. School terms at Oxford University are divided into three: Michaelmas Term in the autumn, Hilary Term from January to March, and Trinity Term from April to June.

Jack's first impressions of college life were recorded in his letters to his father and to Arthur, which he filled with enthusiastic detail. Jack reported to Arthur that Oxford was a dangerous place for a book lover (how much more so for a bibliophile like Jack). He loved the smell of old books, the feel of the paper, and the rich, leather covers of specially bound volumes.

Jack also enjoyed the meals in college. (You may have noticed that food is mentioned a lot in the Narnia books!) Jack preferred plain cooking all of his life and so he enjoyed a full, English breakfast including bacon, eggs, and plenty of toast. Jack loved fish, roast beef and potatoes, lamb chops and good English desserts like summer fruits in heavy cream. However, Jack often ate too fast to fully appreciate the taste of the food he was eating. "I am afraid I gobble," he would often say to friends. In later years, when visiting a pub with a friend, Jack would immediately bellow out to the owner of the pub in his deep, bass voice, "Any pies today?!" Meat pies, one of the specialties of British cuisine, were among Jack's favorite meals.

Jack was most impressed with his first set of rooms at Univ. His first dorm rooms belonged to another student who was on active military service in France. The main room was larger than his father's study at home, filled with dark oak very richly carved, many rugs, a large sofa and several easy chairs. In addition, Jack had an adjoining bedroom. Soon he was moved from this set to his own rooms which, though not as nicely furnished, left space for Jack to add his own things. He especially liked having his own kettle in his room for making tea in the afternoon, always accompanied by his favorite biscuits.

Because of the war, there were only twelve students at Univ at this time. The Hall of the college was being used as a hospital and so was filled with men wounded in the war. In fact, the wounded occupied all the rooms on one of the quads at Univ.[15] Despite this dreary backdrop to his new life, Jack was quite pleased with living at the oldest of the Oxford colleges, especially since it had been the college of one of his favorite poets, Percy

15. A quad consists of a quadrangle of handsomely grown, exquisitely green and perfectly cut grass, usually with a walkway on all four sides and surrounded, also on all four sides, by an interconnected college building, most often consisting of dormitory rooms where the students live.

Bysshe Shelley. Jack particularly enjoyed seeing the statue of Shelley which he passed every morning on the way to the bathroom!

No real reading or study was planned for Jack by his Oxford tutor since he would soon be joining the army. However, since the Oxford tutorial system is so unusual, I had better explain it to you now. This will save time later in the book when we will find Jack himself working as a tutor.

Unlike most other universities, every undergraduate student at Oxford is assigned a tutor. The tutor is called a "fellow" or "don," belongs to one of the colleges, and is usually also a lecturer on his or her subject of expertise. The tutor is perhaps the most important person in a student's life at Oxford. The tutor recommends which lectures the student should attend. He or she assigns reading and, in the case of English, assigns the student a weekly essay topic. An English student, as Jack would later become, brings the assigned essay to his or her tutorial, a weekly meeting with the tutor. The student then reads the essay out loud to the tutor. The tutor makes comments and then gives the student his or her assignment for the next week.

So, at the beginning of Jack's time at Oxford, he was assigned a tutor. That tutor didn't give him any work, however, because Jack was about to enter the army. Despite having no schoolwork, Jack continued his own reading, which included six books in French, Italian and English. Obviously, he did not need the prompting of any tutor to keep him reading great literature.

In his spare time, Jack went rowing on the river during the glorious spring weather of 1917. Oxford is a town built upon two great rivers: the Thames, which flows down to London and thence out to sea, and the smaller Cherwell, well known and loved in Oxfordshire. The Thames, you should know, is called the Isis by all Oxonians. Jack had learned from his roommate at Univ how to row and he made the most of living in a town near two rivers.

On one very lovely Sunday morning in May, rather than attending church service as his father would have liked, Jack bicycled with some fellow students down to the Cherwell River. All the spires of Oxford were gleaming in the sunlight and bells were ringing everywhere. Oxford is a town with a bell in every college tower and there are times when they all ring at once. The sound is so stirring it gives some people goosebumps.

Jack and his friends arrived at a place he would enjoy often throughout his years at Oxford, a spot known as "Parson's Pleasure." This was a place on the Cherwell River that my fellow Virginians would call a "swimming hole." The young college students leapt off their bikes, tore off their clothes, and jumped into the water for a cool, refreshing swim.

ARMY LIFE

Soon enough, Jack was in training to enter the army. His military duties included a lot of marching. Morning parade, as it was called, lasted from 7 to 7:45 a.m., with another parade from 2 to 4. In addition, there were occasional evening lectures on map reading and other subjects. At the beginning of June, Jack joined a cadet battalion and thus moved from the mellow Cotswold stone of Univ to the red-brick and stone monstrosity of Keble College, Oxford for a four-month course on soldiery. Keble was the place I mentioned earlier that has architecture similar to Jack's home church, St. Mark's Dundela. The patterns the architect created by alternating red brick with light brown stone make some people feel dizzy when they look at the buildings of the college!

Jack had a roommate at Keble who changed the course of Jack's life. His name was Edward Francis Courtenay Moore, but his friends called him "Paddy." As you might guess from his nickname, Paddy was an Irishman like Jack. And also like Jack, Paddy had attended one of the best preparatory schools in all of England: Clifton College, Bristol. Paddy was born near Dublin, Ireland, the son of Courtenay Edward Moore and Janie King Moore. Unfortunately, Mr. and Mrs. Moore did not have a happy marriage and they had separated from each other in 1907. Mrs. Moore took Paddy and her young daughter Maureen to live in Bristol, England, as far away from her husband, whom she called "the Beast," as she could get. Mrs. Moore had a brother in Bristol and so that is why she chose that town in which to live. When it was known that Paddy would enter the army through the Oxford Officer Training Corps, Mrs. Moore and Maureen followed Paddy to Oxford, where they decided to live for a time.

Jack eventually met Paddy's mother and sister, thus beginning a friendship with Paddy's whole family. While Jack was in officer training, he spent a good bit of his weekend time at the home of Mrs. Moore. She became like a mother to Jack, who longed for someone to fill the emptiness in his life left by his own mother's death. Thus, Mrs. Moore's house became Jack's home away from home.

Once he entered the cadet battalion, he had no time for reading or writing during the week. His days were filled with digging trenches and marching. Jack's father hoped Jack would be assigned to an artillery unit, rather than the infantry. Albert thought Jack might be safer that way once he entered the war zone since the artillery men are usually further away from the action than those serving in the infantry, who are right on the front lines. However, that didn't work out because of Jack's weakness in mathematics—a core requirement for acceptance into an artillery unit.

Jack did have time to read and write letters on the weekends. In a letter to Arthur Greeves written in June, Jack mentioned for the first time the idea of gathering his own poems together and getting them published as a book. And in another letter in July, he told Arthur he had no patriotic feeling for anything in England except for Oxford, for which he would live and die!

He went home on leave from the army to visit his father in August. Warnie paid a visit home that same month. Then, at the end of the month, the two Lewis brothers were together again, this time in Oxford. It was to be their last time together before the two were shipped off to France as soldiers.

Jack took Responsions again in September and once again he failed the math part. It seems strange that he inherited no mathematics ability whatsoever from his brilliant mother. However, Jack was no longer worried about this failure as he had learned that, once he served for six months in the army, he wouldn't have to take Responsions in order to become a student of the University of Oxford. The University waived this requirement for all young men who served in Britain's armed forces during The Great War.

The day after the Responsions exam, Jack received a temporary assignment in the army, but before beginning his army work he was given a month off. Rather than go to his father's home in Belfast, Jack spent most of his month off with the Moores at their home in Bristol. Obviously, he cared more for the company of the Moores by this time than he did for being with his own father.

At the beginning of October, Jack caught a cold and was sick in bed, but he was happy to be nursed by his adopted mother, Mrs. Moore. While Jack was in Bristol, Paddy learned that he had been assigned to serve in a rifle brigade in France. Before Paddy left for the fighting, he and Jack made a pact. They agreed that if one of them should die in the war, the survivor would look after both Jack's father and Paddy's mother. Soon Paddy left for the killing fields of Europe. Jack wasn't far behind.

On November 15, Jack sent a telegram to Albert saying he would have to report to Southampton on Saturday. This was not good news, for Southampton was the port city of England from which many young men left to fight in the trenches of France. Sadly, Albert never went to see his youngest son off from Southampton. Perhaps Albert misunderstood the telegram. Or maybe he didn't want to leave his work in Belfast. Whatever the reason, this sad mistake on Albert's part, along with Jack's choice of Mrs. Moore as a replacement for his dead mother, eventually led to an almost total breakdown in the relationship between father and son.

Jack got on a ship headed for France on November 17 and he arrived in the trenches on his nineteenth birthday, November 29, 1917. Perhaps you are not old enough yet to have learned very much about trench warfare; if not, a description is in order.

Trench warfare was a form of combat that became a much-used method in The Great War. The two armies fighting each other would dig trenches in the ground from which their different armies could shoot at each other from behind barbed wire. This kind of warfare was used a hundred years ago and more because technology had developed to a point where the military had powerful guns but not as much ability to move their armed forces. The result was a slow and grueling form of defense-oriented fighting. The area between the trench lines of the opposing armies was known as "no-man's land." This area was fully exposed to gunfire from both sides. Attacks, even successful ones, often resulted in many of the combatants being severely wounded or killed.

Another bad thing about trench warfare was that it exposed all the fighters to the quick and easy spread of disease. This was the case because the men not only fought in the trenches but also lived, ate and slept there, breathing in the constant smell of sweat and rotting flesh, for they lived in filthy conditions, often right next to men who were severely wounded or dead. As a result, one common illness that was passed around was trench fever. Jack caught a bad case of it in February 1918. This led to Jack being hospitalized in the British Red Cross Hospital at Le Treport, France. Though glad to be away from the battlefront, Jack feared his return to the trenches once he recovered. He joked, in a letter to Arthur, about the gods hating him. Jack figured the hatred of the gods was natural enough considering his usual treatment of them!

However, it was during this hospital stay that the one true God continued to call out to Jack Lewis, just as Narnia called Shasta to his true north. For it was in the hospital in France that Jack first read a volume of essays by the contemporary Christian author, G. K. Chesterton. At first, Jack simply liked Chesterton's sense of humor. However, as he read more, Jack grew to like Chesterton for his goodness. In reading Chesterton, as in reading MacDonald's *Phantastes*, Jack didn't know what door he was opening in his life. But it was a door through which God's call on Jack's life was becoming ever clearer and louder.

In March, Jack did rejoin his battalion. By the end of the same month, Paddy Moore was killed in action, though this was not confirmed to Mrs. Moore until September. As things turned out, Jack's service in the army was not to last much longer. On April 15, Jack found himself in a tough spot. He was right in the thick of battle, with bombs and gunfire going off all around him. The place was called Mount Bernenchon, and the fighting was later known as the Battle of Arras. As Jack and his comrades were advancing against the enemy, suddenly he was hit from behind by an exploding piece of cannon-fire from his own army. As he went down, he saw his commanding officer fall dead right next to him. All around him, Jack saw both corpses and "horribly smashed men still moving like half-crushed beetles."[16] The moment after Jack was wounded he thought he wasn't breathing and concluded that he was dead. He felt neither fear nor courage. The thought—"here is a man dying"—stood before him as though it was merely a fact he had read in a textbook. But Jack's life was spared, as he was eventually able to crawl back to his comrades where he was picked up by a stretcher-bearer and quickly rushed to the army hospital in Étaples, France.

By May, Jack was well enough to be transferred from the hospital in France to Endsleigh Palace Hospital in London. The pieces of shrapnel in his chest gave him no serious trouble. He made light of the fact that he had brought in about sixty German soldiers as prisoners a day or two prior to being wounded. He reported, "A crowd of enemy soldiers suddenly appeared from nowhere, came out with their hands up, and surrendered."

At the end of June, Jack had the chance to transfer to a different hospital in England in order to continue his physical therapy. He chose a hospital in Bristol so that he could live close to Mrs. Moore. Jack looked back on the events of the previous seven months and gave thanks for his safety and well-being. Many men in his battalion and many of his friends had lost their lives in service to their country.

After the horrible experience of the trenches of Europe and the arduous rehabilitation from his injuries, the rest of 1918 fortunately contained a series of happy events for Jack. In July, he completed the final version of a collection of poems he hoped to send to some book publishers. On November 11, 1918, a peace treaty was signed between the Allies and Germany in a railway carriage in France. And on December 24, Jack was discharged from the hospital in Bristol and honorably discharged from the army at the

---

16. *Surprised by Joy*, chapter 12, p. 196.

same time. Jack immediately traveled home to celebrate Christmas with his father and brother. He arrived at Little Lea on December 27. Despite the fact that Jack and Albert had been estranged, it was a very happy Christmas for the Lewis family. They, along with the rest of the Western world, were simply glad that The Great War was over at last. However, Jack's journey from spiritual slavery to spiritual freedom was just beginning.

7

RESTORATION OF
THE TRUE RELIGION

In his letter to ten-year-old Anne Jenkins written in 1961, C.S. Lewis said that *Prince Caspian*, which follows after *The Horse and His Boy* in Narnian time, was about the "restoration of the true religion after a corruption." In a sense, that was what the next chapter of Jack's life was all about, from 1919 to 1931. Jack had abandoned Christian faith at the age of fourteen when he was a student at Cherbourg School, Great Malvern. That was the "corruption." However, from the age of twenty to the age of thirty-three, Jack went through a gradual process of restoration to the true religion of faith in Jesus Christ. All of this took place while Jack was first a student and later a tutor at Oxford University.

BACK TO OXFORD

By January 1919, Jack was back in Oxford and ready to officially begin his studies as a university student. Jack's chosen course, what American universities would call a "major," was Classical Honour Moderations, a course in Greek and Latin literature. This was the first part of what is called at Oxford "Greats." This course involved the study of Greek and Roman classical literature in the original languages. Right off the bat, Jack had to read two Greek and two Latin authors, plus four Greek plays, and begin the study of Logic. Of course, this was no problem for Jack because he had already studied all of this with the Great Knock.

After a little more than a year of study, Jack took examinations in Classical Honour Mods. On the first day of exams, Jack had a swollen gland in his throat which was very painful. Over the course of the next few days, he experienced one night with practically no sleep at all and could hardly eat anything. Yet, at the end of it all, Jack took a first class degree in Honour Mods; in other words, he got the best grades possible on his exams.

JACK'S FIRST BOOK

At the very beginning of his Oxford studies, Jack also had his first book published. It was called *Spirits in Bondage: A Cycle of Lyrics* and was written under the pen name of Clive Hamilton. Jack had chosen to write under a pen name while still a soldier during The Great War. He was worried about what his fellow officers might think if they found out he wrote poetry. The main theme of these poems was that nature is evil and God, if he exists, is outside of and in opposition to the universe. Some of the poems were written before Jack's service in The Great War, yet they reflect his anger towards any God who would allow the pain and suffering and evil of war to exist. Sadly for Jack, his book of poems received only a few short reviews of little importance.

NEW FRIENDS

Jack's time as a student at Oxford University was important not only for the books he read and the lectures he attended but also for the lifelong friends he made. One of the first great friends of his student days was Leo Baker, a student at Wadham College. (This college was known, at one time, for having the oldest tree in Oxford in its Fellows' Garden.) Together, Jack and Leo put together a collection of poems which they hoped to have published by Basil Blackwell, owner of Blackwell's Bookshop. The collection was never published. But it was Baker who introduced Jack to another man who would become a lifelong friend: Owen Barfield, also of Wadham. Jack later described Barfield as a friend who shared all his interests but looked at them from a completely different angle. The subsequent commitment of Barfield and another friend, A. C. Harwood, to belief in the supernatural brought a great shock to Jack; he had thought these friends, at least, to be safe from such "superstitions," as he called them. In the long run both friends, especially Barfield, caused Jack to reconsider his atheism.

Moving Toward God

At the beginning of Trinity Term, 1920, Jack moved from his college rooms into a house with the Moores who had decided to move from Bristol to Oxford to be near him. The house was in Headington, two miles east of the center of Oxford. Jack began the second part of "Greats" which included work with two tutors, one for philosophy, E. F. Carritt, and one for history, George Hope Stevenson. Once again, Jack's previous studies in classical Greek and Roman philosophy and history were standing him in good stead. He had only to go over in more careful detail ground already covered.

Through studying philosophy, Jack came to the point of believing that there must be some kind of God. However, he thought that human beings still knew nothing for certain about this deity. Jack had moved from atheism (a belief in no God) to agnosticism (the belief that there might be a God), and then to a belief, as he called it, in the Absolute.

In 1921, Jack wrote an 11,000-word essay on the topic of Optimism. This English essay won the Chancellor's Prize in May 1921. As a result, Jack was invited to read part of his essay at Encaenia. Encaenia is the June ceremony of the University of Oxford at which honorary degrees are awarded to distinguished people, and benefactors of the university are remembered. Encaenia is a very formal affair, with all the faculty of the university wearing their colorful academic gowns. The event takes place within the honey-colored walls of the Sheldonian Theatre. This horseshoe-shaped building, with its gorgeous painted ceiling depicting the *Triumph of Religion, Arts and Science over Envy, Hate and Malice*, was designed by the famous architect Sir Christopher Wren. George Friedrich Handel, composer of the *Messiah*, was one of the first great composers to perform in the Sheldonian.

So imagine Jack, on this most formal occasion, stepping up to the podium to read his prize-winning essay, and guess what happened? Something we all fear when we have to walk across a stage in front of a crowd—Jack tripped and fell down! He did get back up again and he did read his essay. Once he got over the embarrassment of falling down, the reading went rather well. In the essay itself, Jack dealt with the question of God; he tried to prove, at least to himself, that it really didn't matter whether there was a God or not.

Jack's thoughts about God at this time were influenced by several things. One was Jack's conversation and correspondence with his friend, Leo Baker. In a letter to Baker around this time, Jack said that blind faith was unsuitable for people like Baker and himself who knew too much and saw life too widely. Jack believed the biblical view of the universe was too comfortable; he believed in using reason to develop his own world-view, even if the end result was meaninglessness. Jack wrote that the trouble with God is that he is like someone who never answers your letters, so in time you come to the conclusion, either that God does not exist, or that you have his address wrong.

A second influence on Jack's beliefs about God was his desire to steer clear of all spiritualism. In March of 1921, he had a couple of meetings with the man who had been his favorite poet, fellow Irishman W. B. Yeats. Jack was bothered by Yeats's interest in magic. Some of Jack's other contacts with spiritualists also scared him away from any dabbling in the occult.

A third influence was the death of William Kirkpatrick in the spring of that same year. Jack told his father that he owed to Kirk as much as one person could owe to another human being, at least intellectually. Kirk's death raised for Jack, once again, the whole question of life after death. Jack said he wasn't really interested in immortality. However, the difference between the living Kirk and the mere body left behind at death made it impossible for Jack to believe that the real person he had known had suddenly turned into nothing.

THE END OF "GREATS" AND BEGINNING OF ENGLISH

By the end of 1921, Jack was looking forward to finishing Greats; he hoped that he would also soon be finished with financial dependence upon his father. That, however, was not to be the case quite yet.

In May of 1922, Jack began to discuss with his father his future options. One of his tutors suggested that he stay on at Oxford for another year after Greats and take another school, that is, another subject. The tutor suggested that if Jack did so, Univ would almost certainly continue his scholarship. The obvious choice of another school for Jack was English literature, a rising and fairly new subject at Oxford at that time. The thought behind this suggestion was that if Jack was able to get a first or second class degree in Greats and a first in English the following year, he would be in an excellent position for obtaining a fellowship, that is, a teaching job, at Oxford. Albert soon told Jack, "I heartily approve of you taking another school and I will be happy to pay for your further education."

From June 8 to 14, Jack took his examination in the second half of Greats. This involved six hours of writing every day for six days. On July 28, Jack had an oral examination and on August 4 he learned that he had received a first class degree, thus becoming a Bachelor of Arts. Jack immediately sent a telegram to his father telling him the good news.

In October, Jack started on his English course. His English tutor was F. P. Wilson, later one of the editors of the *Oxford History of English Literature*, who would one day invite Jack to contribute the volume on the 16th century to that series. One of the first things Jack did in his study of English literature was to attend George Gordon's discussion class, which he found very exciting. It was there that he also made a new friend in fellow student Nevill Coghill. However, there was a shock in store for Jack; Coghill was, in addition to being the most intelligent and best-informed student in the class, a Christian.

This disturbing fact about Coghill joined with a larger disturbance Jack was encountering in his reading. He was beginning to find, through his English studies, that all the authors he enjoyed the most had Christianity in common.

Even among ancient authors, it was the most religious ones that he found most satisfying. On the other hand, the authors he should have been in agreement with because of their atheism, he found to be most lacking in depth.

Because Jack had decided to try to cram the three-year English program into only one year, before he knew it he was taking his final examination in English language and literature. This involved a full five days of testing on everything from Old English to the literature of the 19th century. On the last day of exams, Jack found out the Exeter College job he had been hoping to get had gone to someone else, causing him to feel terribly let down. He also thought he had done poorly on a number of the English papers. Jack's performance on his oral exam in English, however, gave him back his confidence and he came away slightly more encouraged.

Then, to his surprise, Jack learned that he and his friend Nevill Coghill were the only students that year to receive first class degrees in English Language and Literature. Once again, Jack immediately sent a telegram to his father telling him the great news—"A First in English."

As impressive as it was, Jack's Triple First at Oxford did not immediately obtain him a teaching position at the university as he had hoped. Thus 1924 began as a difficult year for Jack. He was continuing to apply for every Oxford fellowship for which he was qualified, but without any positive response. In addition, his scholarship at University College had run out, so he was forced to ask his father Albert for more financial help. In order to enhance his qualifications for a fellowship, Jack continued his studies with the thought that he might get an additional degree.

A Temporary Job

In May of 1924, Jack received some good news. His former philosophy tutor, E. F. Carritt, was going to America to teach philosophy for a year. Jack was asked by the Master of University College if he would undertake Carritt's tutorials and give some lectures in philosophy during Carritt's absence. Jack would be allowed to pursue a permanent placement at the same time. The job paid only £200 per year, but it got Jack's foot in the door for an Oxford fellowship. He immediately wrote to his father telling him the good news and informing him, once again, that he would still need some financial help from home.

Jack accepted the position and immediately began preparing by going over all the "Greats" reading he had already done as a student, this time with a view toward teaching the material as a tutor. Jack was concerned about the lectures, which would require fourteen hours of talking for the whole term. He told his father that he could probably tell the world everything he knew in five hours! Jack worked hard throughout the summer of 1924 writing notes for each of his lectures. He had as his goal to learn, right from the beginning, how to talk to students and not merely read a lecture.

Tuesday, October 14, 1924 at 10 a.m. was the day and hour of C.S. Lewis's first lecture at Oxford University. He spoke on the subject of "The Good, its position among values." Unfortunately, he was scheduled to speak at the same time as a much older and more popular teacher at the university, and the announcement for Jack's lecture gave the wrong location. In the end, only four people showed up for Jack's first appearance as a university teacher.

A Full-Time Job

By the end of his yearlong appointment, Jack was getting nervous about getting a permanent job. But in April of 1925, a Fellowship in English was announced at Magdalen College, Oxford. Jack applied for it but was not too hopeful of getting the job after being rejected for so many other positions.

However, this time Jack was not disappointed. He was invited to dinner at Magdalen College "under inspection." After the dinner, the President of Magdalen, Sir Thomas Herbert Warren, asked to meet with Jack privately. Warren asked Jack, "Would you be willing to tutor students in philosophy, in addition to English?" Jack later told his father, "I would have been willing to tutor a flock of performing birds in the college quad if Magdalen would give me a job!"

The next day Jack got a phone call asking him to come to Magdalen. When he entered the college, he was met by the President who said, "Mr. Lewis, Magdalen College has elected you as a Fellow and Tutor in English Language and Literature!" The pay began at £500 per year with provision of rooms, a pension, and a dining allowance. Thrilled, Jack immediately sent a telegram to his father. An announcement of Jack's new job appeared in *The Times* on May 22. Then Jack wrote a more detailed letter to his father, thanking him for his undying support over the past six years which had helped him to succeed in the end.

Magdalen College assigned to Jack the white-paneled college rooms which he would live in for the next twenty-nine years: Staircase III, Number 3, of New Building—new in 1733, that is! To Jack's great surprise, he found out that he would have to fully furnish the rooms himself. Carpets, tables, curtains, chairs, fenders, fire irons, coal boxes, table covers, and other furniture cost him £90 altogether. And that was a lot of money in 1925!

Jack's surroundings at Magdalen were beautiful beyond belief. From his large sitting room, he could look out upon the Magdalen deer park with nothing to remind him that he was in a town. His smaller sitting room and bedroom had a stunning view of the fifteenth-century tower and sand-colored Cloisters of Magdalen. Within a minute of sitting at his desk, Jack could be stretching his legs down Addison's Walk beside the Cherwell River.

Jack didn't know it then, but there was to be an important walk along the Cherwell River that would soon lead to restoration of the faith he had lost as a teenager. In the next chapter, we will meet the new friends who joined Jack and helped him along his spiritual pilgrimage.

Jack's mother, Flora Lewis

Little Lea as it looks today

Dunluce Castle, the real Cair Paravel?

Jack & Warnie with their bikes

c.1909 | *Warnie, Albert & Jack*

Campbell College

Malvern College

1919 | Jack

1920 | Jack's tutor W. T. Kirkpatrick
with his wife at Gastons

High Street, Oxford

Parson's Pleasure, Oxford

1927 | *Jack, Maureen & Janie King Moore vacationing in Cornwall in September*

The front of The Kilns as it looks today

The Common Room of The Kilns as it looks today

Holy Trinity Church, Headington Quarry

Magdalen College Tower, Oxford

Magdalen Dining Hall

New Building, Magdalen College (Jack had his rooms on the second floor near the center)

Magdalen Cloister

Addison's Walk

The Eagle and Child pub, where
the Inklings met every Tuesday

1949 | Jack & Warnie

The Eastgate Hotel, where Jack
and Joy first met

Jack with his stepsons, David &
Douglas Gresham

1997 | Douglas Gresham in front of
10 Old High Street

1960 | Jack's wife, Helen Joy Davidman

The Old Inn, Crawfordsburn,
where Jack & Joy honeymooned
in Northern Ireland

Joy's Memorial,
Oxford Crematorium

Trinity Street, Cambridge

Magdalene College, Cambridge

Magdalene College Chapel

The C.S. Lewis Memorial Sculpture, Holywood Arches Library, Belfast, Northern Ireland by Sculptor Ross Wilson

Author Will Vaus & family in front of the Browneshill Dolmen ("Stone Table"), County Carlow, Republic of Ireland

8

ALMOST A PROFESSOR

Most people would think of Jack's new job at Magdalen College as being that of a professor. However, he wasn't a professor yet. Jack was a tutor, also called a don or a fellow. As a tutor, Jack would give lectures in the university and he had to do some very hard work professors did not have to do. For the next thirty years, Jack would be tutoring students in English literature. This meant that he would meet with students, usually by twos or threes, almost every weekday in term time. He would assign reading and essay topics, listen to and critique their essays on English literature, and tell his students what lectures to attend. It was quite a workload Jack was taking on, but he looked forward to it with keen anticipation.

Over the years Jack tutored a number of students who later became famous. One of these was a man by the name of John Betjeman, who became Poet Laureate of England. One day Betjeman showed up for his tutorial with Jack wearing a pair of eccentric bedroom slippers. Betjeman said, "I hope you don't mind. I'm wearing these because I have a blister."

Jack replied, "I would mind them very much if *I* had to wear them, but I don't mind *you* wearing them at all!"

Unfortunately Betjeman, like a number of other students Jack tutored, was not very diligent, and so he eventually left Oxford without a degree. Somehow that didn't seem to harm Betjeman's career as a poet. Though he and Jack didn't get along too well when Jack was his tutor, they reconciled with each other in later life.

LIFE AS AN ENGLISH TUTOR

In January 1926, Jack gave his first lecture in the English School. He modestly selected the smallest lecture room at Magdalen College, only to have a crowd of undergraduates in attendance, proving too large for the room. Jack played the pied piper as he led his students across the High Street, suspending traffic, en route to a bigger lecture hall.

A typical day during term time would begin with Jack being awakened at 7:30 by his scout bringing him hot water for washing and shaving. In those days every college staircase had a scout, or servant, who would tend to the needs of students and faculty members on that staircase. And in Jack's time at Magdalen, the residents of New Building had to go outside of their building to use a toilet. One student who was an undergraduate at Magdalen when Jack was a fellow there remembers passing him every morning on the way to the bathroom!

After attending to issues of personal hygiene, Jack would go for a stroll along Addison's Walk; this circular path hugs the banks of the Cherwell River at points and on the far side there is a spectacular view of Magdalen Tower in the distance. When going for a stroll along Addison's Walk, it can seem like you are living back in the 16th century; one is so far removed from the hustle and bustle of the modern-day Oxford High Street. Jack loved this walk for that very reason.

After his walk, Jack would take breakfast in the Senior Common Room at 8 o'clock. Years later, when he became a Christian, Jack would attend chapel service from 8 to 8:15. From 9 to 1 o'clock Jack would usually tutor various students. In the afternoon, he would ride his bicycle or take the bus out to the house he shared with the Moores, "Hillsboro," in Headington. There he had lunch, took the dog for a walk, and helped Mrs. Moore with household chores. In the evening, Jack returned to college where, as a benefit of his job, he would enjoy a free dinner in hall. After dinner, the dons would retreat to the Senior Common Room to enjoy after-dinner drinks, fruit and nuts. However, Jack did not go to the Common Room more than two or three times per week. He had too many other evening clubs and reading to keep him busy.

Jack's reading in 1926 included G. K. Chesterton, whom he considered to be the most sensible man alive, apart from his Christianity. Sometime early in 1926, he read Chesterton's book, *The Everlasting Man*. For the first time, he saw the whole Christian outline of history in a way that seemed to make sense. Jack was beginning to lose the spiritual chess game he was playing. He would later put *The Everlasting Man* on his Top Ten List of books which did the most to help guide his philosophy of life.

On May 1, 1926, Jack participated for the first time in the Magdalen May Day celebration. At this event, the Magdalen choirboys ring in the spring season by singing from the top of Magdalen Tower at six o'clock in the morning! This is accompanied by much merry-making down on the street, including people jumping from Magdalen Bridge and from punts—long, narrow, flat-bottomed boats—into the Cherwell River! Also during the merry month of May, 1926, Jack met a man who would become a life-long friend—John Ronald Reuel Tolkien—then Professor of Anglo-Saxon at Oxford. The two men met at one of Jack's first English faculty meetings. Jack didn't know it then, but his friendship with Tolkien would lead him to spiritual checkmate.

In September, Jack had another literary achievement. His epic poem *Dymer* was published by J. M. Dent under the name Clive Hamilton. Once again, Jack used a pen name because he didn't want it known broadly around Oxford that he was writing poems. According to Jack, this poem was about a man who begets a monster. The monster turns around and kills the man and then becomes a god.

Jack and his brother Warnie spent the Christmas holiday of 1926 with their father. They didn't know it then, but it was to be the last time all three of them would be together as a family. Albert wrote in his diary that it was a very happy holiday: "Roses all the way." Soon Warnie sailed for China to continue his military service there.

When he was back at Oxford, Jack spent many mornings in the Bodleian Library working on the writing of a book that would become *English*

Literature in the Sixteenth Century. Jack would often sit in Duke Humfrey's Library, the oldest part of the Bodleian, dating to the 15th century. There he would order the books he wished to study, and they would be brought to him from the "dungeon" of the Library somewhere underground. Jack would then sit and read in his "box" between the shelves of ancient chained books. To Jack's left was a little leaded window looking down into the garden of Exeter College. Far above him was a painted ceiling, containing the crest of the University of Oxford. The motto on the crest reads: "Dominus Illuminatio Mea." This is the Latin for the first line of Psalm 27, "The Lord is my light." The only bad thing about all this beauty and ancient grandeur was that it would often weave a spell over Jack that easily led him to daydream rather than study!

The Most Reluctant Convert

While Jack was deep in his study of sixteenth century literature, he was also continuing along on his personal spiritual journey at a rapid pace. A turning point took place for Jack on top of a double-decker bus riding home from college one day. Red double-decker buses, such as you find mostly in England, are great fun to ride. When sitting on the top level of the bus you have a grand view over everything, even over some rooftops around you.

However, on this particular day, Jack was not noticing the view outside the bus. He was looking deep within his own soul. As he gazed inside himself, he suddenly realized he was holding something or someone at arm's length. At the same time, he recognized that he could either shut or open the door of his life to this something or to this someone. In that moment, on top of the double-decker, going up Headington Hill, Jack chose to open a spiritual door in his life.

Jack later said he felt like the icy cold nature of his former unbelief was beginning to thaw. He felt like a snowman with the ice starting to melt at his back—drip, drip, drip, and then trickle, trickle. It was just like the Witch's winter turning to spring thaw in Narnia, once Aslan was on the move. The ice in Jack's heart began to melt as God got closer to him, or as he got closer to God.

After that important ride on the double-decker, Jack tried to obey his conscience every day. He also examined his soul to bring himself into harmony with what he then called "universal Spirit." Upon examination, he found that his life was filled with lust, ambition, fear and hatred. He said he felt like the demon-possessed man in the Gospels whose name was Legion. In his attempt to obey his conscience, Jack found he could not get through one hour without asking God for help. Jack knew he could no longer escape the presence of the Almighty. So one day in the spring of 1929, he knelt down in his room at Magdalen College and gave control of his life to God. He felt like "the most dejected and reluctant convert in all England"!

ALBERT'S DEATH

The second most important event in Jack's life in 1929 was the sickness and death of his father in the autumn of that year. Jack spent most of August and September at home in Belfast nursing Albert. During these days Jack was troubled by the fact that he had so little love for his father, though he cared for his father's physical needs most dutifully. At the same time, looking so much like his father, Jack felt he was losing part of himself as his father's life was slipping away.

In mid-September, an operation revealed that Albert had colon cancer. Following the advice of the doctors, who told Jack that his father might live for some time, Jack returned to Oxford on September 22. However, Jack received news two days later that his father's condition had worsened. He immediately returned to Belfast, but his father died while Jack was still on the way home. Albert's funeral took place in the family church, St. Mark's Dundela. Warnie was not present during Albert's illness, death or funeral, as he was kept in China on military service.

Following Albert's death, Jack learned that Warnie would not be able to come home for another few months. Thus Jack was left to settle his father's estate by himself. It was only after Albert's death that Jack began to realize how much he was going to miss his father. Jack wrote to Warnie commenting on how his father used to "fill a room" even though physically he was not a very big man. Now that Jack had total freedom in his childhood home, that liberty became detestable to him.

Perhaps the one place where Jack most felt the loss of his father was in his letter writing. Since school days, Jack had been exchanging letters regularly with Albert, often weekly. To whom was Jack to write now that his father was dead? Jack's letters to Arthur Greeves filled the gap. The communication between these two friends, which had fallen off for a time, was now resumed with great energy. In July of 1930, Jack wrote to Arthur saying there were a great many subjects on which Arthur was the only person to whom he could write, the only person who would understand. He told Arthur that the common ground they shared represented the deepest core of his life.

FRIENDS ALONG THE ROAD

One of the things Jack wrote to Arthur about was the friends who were helping him along his spiritual journey; one of these friends was Alan Griffiths. Griffiths was a former English student with whom Jack kept in close contact. Like Jack, Griffiths was on a journey toward Christian faith. Griffiths later wrote about Jack: "... it was through him that my mind was gradually brought back to Christianity."

Another important friend along this stage of the journey was Hugo Dyson, a teacher of English at Reading. Having met him once, Jack determined to get to know him better and so invited him for an overnight stay in his college rooms. Jack wrote to Arthur that Dyson was a man who loved the truth, one who made literary activities dependent upon religion and philosophy.

Jack also wrote to Arthur about his own spiritual progress. Though Jack sometimes felt like he wasn't making headway, he still tried to do those things which might lead him forward. One of those outward acts was attendance at morning chapel in college. He began to attend chapel during the Michaelmas Term of 1930. It must be understood that Jack was not yet a Christian. His conversion, mentioned above, was only to theism. He had become a believer in God, but not yet a believer in Jesus as God's Son. Even though he wasn't yet a Christian, Jack felt it was important to "fly the flag" of his new commitment to God in some way. Thus he began to attend chapel in college and worship services on Sunday at his parish church.

In Jack's outer life, one of the big events of 1930 was his brother Warnie's return from China. Warnie left Shanghai en route to Great Britain on February 24. His trip home included stops in Japan and the United States. He arrived back in England on April 16. He had been away from home exactly three years and five days.

The Kilns

Warnie had only been home for a few months when he and Jack decided to buy a house, along with Mrs. Moore, in Headington Quarry. The house was called The Kilns because of the abandoned brick kilns then on the property. On a warm July day, Jack and Warnie went to see the outside of the two-story red brick house with red tile roof for the first time. It was at the end of a little-used road, offering them much privacy. Situated at the bottom of Shotover Hill, the house was surrounded by an eight-acre garden with a hard tennis court and woods beyond that. In the midst of the woods was a pond where Jack would eventually take a daily swim in good weather. The story was told that the poet Shelley used to sail paper boats in that very same pond. Both Jack and Warnie were delighted with the whole place.

Jack, Mrs. Moore and Warnie bought the house for £3300 and moved in on October 10. Jack described the house, in a letter to Arthur, as having a "good night atmosphere." He concluded that good life must have been lived there before them. This was quite a contrast to Jack's feeling about Little Lea, a house that had been "well suffered in."

In January 1931, Jack and Warnie took their first walking tour together. This journey was what we Americans would call a hiking or backpacking vacation. The trip took Jack and Warnie through Wales. After seeing the famous ruins of Tintern Abbey, Jack wrote in a letter to Arthur: "All churches should be roofless. A holier place I never saw." Around this time, Jack happily learned that Warnie had also come around to thinking that the religious view of things was true. They started attending church together at Holy Trinity, Headington Quarry—a stone's throw from The Kilns.

Jack Returns to Christian Faith

The most important event of Jack's entire life took place just a year after the Lewises and the Moores moved into The Kilns, in September 1931. On the third weekend of that month, Hugo Dyson came to stay with Jack in his rooms at Magdalen. J. R. R. Tolkien joined them on Saturday evening and they ended up talking until 3 a.m. The conversation began in Addison's Walk shortly after dinner and was focused on the topic of myth. They were interrupted by a rush of wind and the fall of autumn leaves around them, which filled each man with a sense of awe. The talk continued in Jack's rooms and drifted from Christianity to the difference between love and friendship and then back to poetry and books. When Tolkien left at 3 a.m., Jack and Dyson continued talking for another hour, striding up and down the cloister of New Building.

Their discussion of Christianity focused on the idea of redemption. Jack asked his friends, "How could the life and death of Jesus Christ have saved the world?" Dyson and Tolkien pointed out: "Jack, you like the idea of sacrifice in a pagan story. The myths of the dying and rising god enthrall you. Now the story of Christ is simply a true myth. It is a myth which works on the soul in the same way as the pagan myths but with this big difference: it really happened!"

This discussion convinced Jack that the Christian story was to be approached in the same imaginative way as the pagan myths. He also felt that the Christian story was full of meaning. Finally, as a result of his conversation with Dyson and Tolkien, Jack was nearly certain that the story of Christ really happened in the way described in the Gospels.

Eight days later, Jack went on a motorcycle journey, riding in Warnie's sidecar, to Whipsnade Zoo, not far from Oxford. Imagine Jack in goggles, bumping along in the sidecar of a motorcycle, hurtling down a country road, autumn leaves falling all around in the golden light of September. When he and Warnie started out for Whipsnade, Jack did not believe that Jesus Christ was the Son of God; but when they reached the zoo, he did. On October 1st, Jack wrote to Arthur telling him that he had just passed from believing in God to definitely believing in Christ. He mentioned that his long talk with Dyson and Tolkien had a lot to do with his return to Christian belief. Though Jack was not yet a professor of English, as I pointed out at the beginning of this chapter, he had become a professor of true faith in Jesus Christ.

What was it about the ride to Whipsnade Zoo that changed Jack's mind about Christianity? Jack later said that he spent that motorcycle journey neither in deep thought nor in great emotion. The experience of conversion for Jack was more like the experience of lying motionless in bed after a long sleep and suddenly becoming aware that he was awake. On the trip to Whipsnade, Jack woke up, spiritually speaking, and realized he was a Christian!

By the end of 1931, Tolkien was dropping in on Jack every Monday morning at Magdalen for a drink and a talk. These weekly meetings were the first glimmers of what would become known as the literary group "The Inklings." And by the end of the year, Warnie was back in China for another tour of duty. On Christmas Day, thousands of miles away from each other, both Jack and Warnie attended church and took Communion for the first time as real believers. The true religion had indeed been restored after a corruption in both Jack's and Warnie's lives. Little did they know it then, but Jack's return to faith in Christ would change the world.

9

THE SPIRITUAL LIFE

The book *The Voyage of the Dawn Treader*, according to C.S. Lewis, is all about the spiritual life, seen especially in the character and adventures of Reepicheep, the valiant mouse. In September 1931, at the age of 32, Jack Lewis returned to a spiritual life and began a relationship with Jesus Christ. As a result, the second half of his life was dramatically different from the first half. For the rest of his life he was sailing toward Aslan's country.

Jack once said that his reacceptance of the Christian faith was the beginning of reaching outside himself; in the same way, conversion was the beginning of the end of selfishness in the life of Eustace Clarence Scrubb in *The Voyage of the Dawn Treader*. You may remember that, in that story, Eustace kept a diary for a while. In that diary he wrote down all the ways in which he thought he wasn't being treated right. After Eustace was turned into a dragon, he became more interested in helping other people. And after Aslan turned Eustace back into a real boy again, Eustace gave up his habit of keeping a journal.

The same was true of Jack. After his return to Christianity, he gave up what he called the time-wasting habit of keeping a diary. On purpose, he no longer took any particular interest in himself. Now that he was a committed Christian, Jack was much more interested in other people. He began to reach out in a number of ways, beginning in the 1930s and throughout the rest of his life.

READING

One way that Jack got out of himself was through reading great books. You might wonder how reading helped Jack to become less self-centered. Jack later explained: "In reading great literature I become a thousand men and yet remain myself. Like the night sky in the Greek poem I see with myriad eyes, but it is still I who see. Here, as in worship, in love, in moral action, and in knowing, I transcend myself; and am never more myself than when I do."[17] Jack said he wished he could see through the eyes of a bee or smell through the nose of a dog. However, since neither bees nor dogs could write books, Jack had to content himself with books written by human beings!

One book to which Arthur Greeves introduced him would spur Jack to write, not just one book, but a whole series of books. The book which Arthur recommended to Jack was David Lindsay's *Voyage to Arcturus*. Lindsay's book inspired Jack to write his own science fiction books. Jack suddenly realized, "I can smuggle Christian ideas into fiction!"

In 1937, Jack wrote *Out of the Silent Planet*, the first novel in his science fiction trilogy. Like most of Jack's fiction, *Out of the Silent Planet* is a story of good against evil. Dr. Elwin Ransom is on the side of the good. He is kidnapped by two men named Weston and Devine and taken by spaceship to the planet Malacandra, which humans call Mars. Weston and Devine plan to offer Ransom as a sacrifice to the inhabitants of Malacandra and then take over the planet for the human race.

Jack smuggled the good news about Jesus Christ into this story by telling the Gospel from the perspective of the Malacandrians. Toward the end of the book, Ransom is taken to the Oyarsa, or angel, of Malacandra. The Oyarsa explains that Earth, like all the planets, once had an Oyarsa but that this Oyarsa became "bent." It was this Oyarsa's plan to spoil other planets in addition to his own. To prevent this, Maleldil (God) drove this bent

---

17. C.S. Lewis, *An Experiment in Criticism*, New York: Cambridge University Press, 1961, p. 141.

Oyarsa out of heaven and bound him in the atmosphere of Earth. Thus Earth became the "silent planet," out of touch with the rest of the universe. The Oyarsa of Malacandra tells Ransom that there are stories among the Oyarses that Maleldil dared terrible things, wrestling with the Bent One in Thulcandra (Earth).

THE PILGRIM'S REGRESS

Through his writing, Jack found another way to reach outside himself, and after coming back to Christ, he wrote with even greater fervor. Up until this point in his life, Jack's ambition had been to become a famous poet. However, once his life was committed to following Christ, the desire grew within him to use his writing skills to help other people, rather than to gain renown for himself. Ironically, once Jack's reason for writing changed, he did eventually become very famous, but for other forms of literature, not poetry.

The first book Jack wrote to help others come to faith in Jesus Christ was composed while he was on holiday with his friend Arthur Greeves in Belfast. In the summer of 1932, Jack stayed at Bernagh, the Greeves' family home, across the street from Little Lea. "Arthur," he said, "I've got an idea for a story. I want to tell my own spiritual journey but put it in the form of an allegory."

An allegory is a story in which everything in the imaginative world of the story represents something in real life. For example, a giant might represent despair, or a mountain might represent the home of God.

Jack described his new book as an "up-to-date" version of John Bunyan's *Pilgrim's Progress*. The first edition contained Jack's Mappa Mundi on the end papers; this was a map of the fictional world Jack created in the book. *The Pilgrim's Regress* received a number of good reviews but unfortunately, only 650 out of the first 1,000 copies printed were actually sold. Jack took this failure in stride; now that he was a dedicated Christian, he no longer seemed as concerned about his own success or failure.

SCHOLARLY WRITING

Fiction was not the only thing Jack was writing in the 1930s. He was also writing books about English literature. In the winter of 1935, Jack was invited to contribute the volume on the 16th century to the planned *Oxford History of English Literature*. He at first said "no" to this request, but then accepted the invitation of his former tutor, F. P. Wilson. In order to write this book, Jack read everything written in English in the 16th century! It is no wonder he called this book "Oh Hell!" after the initials O. H. E. L., standing for Oxford History of English Literature!

In other literary news, Jack reported to Arthur in December 1935 that he had completed writing what was to be *The Allegory of Love*. This was Jack's first scholarly book to be published and one which made him famous as a teacher of English literature. As the title suggests, the book was all about allegory and medieval love poetry.

LETTERS

You would think that someone who spent most of his adult life writing books wouldn't want to spend any of his free time writing anything else. But Jack did! He said that writing was like an itch—it had to be scratched. And so another way Jack reached out to others after his return to faith was through letter writing. At first, his letters were only written to close friends and family members. But eventually Jack's correspondence came to include people from all over the globe.

In his letters to his brother and to Arthur Greeves, Jack began to discuss various topics related to Christianity. They discussed the doctrine of the atonement, how we are made "at one" with God through the death and resurrection of Jesus. In a letter to his brother, Jack discussed the place of the sacraments within Christianity, specifically the sacrament called The Lord's Supper or Holy Communion. When Jack first became a Christian, he only took the bread and wine at church once per month. But toward the end of his life, Communion became so meaningful that he wanted to have it every week. As Jack would later discover, and also picture in a beautiful way in Aslan's Table on Ramandu's Island, eating the bread and drinking the wine of Communion is a wonderful way God has given us to grow in our relationship with Jesus.

In his letters to Warnie and Arthur, Jack also discussed the subject of prayer. When Arthur asked Jack to pray for him, Jack immediately wrote back saying, "I do." Jack wasn't sure if his prayers did any good for his friend, but he was sure it was good for him. Jack realized he couldn't pray for change in Arthur without seeing the same needs in himself. Making prayer an everyday part of his life helped Jack to become more humble. In the years to come, Jack would often write to friends assuring them that he prayed for them, even when waking in the middle of the night.

By the end of 1932, Warnie returned to England for good from the Far East, and he soon retired from the Royal Army Service Corps. Warnie moved into The Kilns permanently and a wing was added to the house to make room for him. Jack was thrilled. While this meant the end of letter writing between Jack and Warnie, once Jack became a famous author, Warnie would help him in responding to the hundreds of people who wrote to him every year.

Also in the 1930s, Jack began what would become a long correspondence with an Anglican nun of the Community of St. Mary the Virgin in Wantage, England, not far from Oxford. Her name was Sister Penelope and she wrote to Jack after reading *Out of the Silent Planet*. Sister Penelope was also an author and a number of her books gave Jack ideas for his own writing.

TEACHING

Writing books and letters was only one part of Jack's everyday life. The main part of his life was filled with teaching. Jack took a very personal interest in how his students were doing, especially how they fared in exams. On one occasion, Jack wrote to one of his students, Mary Shelley Neylan, who had received a fourth class degree in English. Jack tried to comfort Mary by telling her that her real quality as a student was so much better than what showed through in her final exams. Mary Shelley Neylan was so encouraged by the words of her former tutor that she wrote to Jack often. After many years of correspondence, Jack was able to lead Mary to personal faith in Jesus Christ.

However, Jack was very careful not to use his teaching time to evangelize his students. He didn't think that would be right. If a student asked him a question about Christian faith, Jack would give the best answer he could. Otherwise, he would let his students discover faith on their own. Jack said that his position as an English teacher did not allow him to teach the most important things like Christian doctrine. However, he felt there was honest work for him to do as a teacher of English literature: the work of helping students to get rid of wrong mental habits, and the work of teaching logic—just like the professor in *The Lion, the Witch and the Wardrobe*! On the whole, Jack felt like he was becoming a better person through being a tutor. He was also grateful for the friends he made among each group of students.

EVERYDAY LIFE

Jack's life was very full of teaching and writing books and letters. Nevertheless, because he was so organized in the use of his time, he also made room in his life for family, friends and fun.

One of the truly remarkable things about Jack was that he cared for Mrs. Moore as if she were his own mother. This caring relationship began, as you will remember, when Mrs. Moore's son was killed in The Great War. Jack had made a promise to Paddy that he would care for his mother and he was going to see it through to the end, for he knew that the God whom he chose to serve commanded faithfulness. As he once commented to his brother about living with Mrs. Moore, "I have definitely chosen and don't regret the choice."

The choice to care for Mrs. Moore would have a deep effect on the rest of Jack's life, both positive and negative. As one of Jack's friends, George Sayer, pointed out, Mrs. Moore brought to Jack a sense of settled home life and hospitality which otherwise would have been unknown. She taught Jack how to do simple household things like making marmalade. From Mrs. Moore Jack learned to be generous and care for other people. But on the negative side, Mrs. Moore's constant presence in Jack's life was a bit of an obstacle to him getting married. So long as Jack's adopted "mother" was still in the picture, marriage seemed unthinkable.

Still, Jack enjoyed his home life, such as it was. And in the early '30s, Jack especially enjoyed the fact that his brother Warnie was settling into life at The Kilns, keeping active with much gardening and reading. On Sunday nights, Warnie would play one of Beethoven's symphonies on his gramophone for his brother and Mrs. Moore. On other nights Jack enjoyed a delightful time reading—especially the new children's story which his friend Tolkien had just written: *The Hobbit*. Jack described the book in a letter to Arthur as precisely the kind of book either of them would have longed to read or write when they were teenagers.

JACK ON VACATION

Everything Jack did, he performed with gusto! This was especially true of holidays. After grading exams one summer, Jack took off with his brother Warnie on a journey to the coastal town of Helensburgh, Scotland to see their uncles. While the time with their relations was enjoyable, the brothers most appreciated the special time they were able to spend alone together. Jack and Warnie loved getting away from the busyness of the town to hike over the mountains between Loch Long and Loch Lomond. The Lewis brothers reveled in their exploration of the countryside, with its breathtaking views and crisp, cool air. Jack could easily imagine the heavy shapes of rock which formed the mountain summits being the fastnesses of giants. During one of their hikes, Jack and Warnie shared a glorious hour bathing in a golden brown mountain stream, putting their heads under a waterfall, and sitting beside the stream to eat sandwiches after their swim.

Jack also loved holidays with the Moores. One springtime, Mrs. Moore and her daughter Maureen took off with Jack by car across England, and then on the ferry to Ireland. Jack celebrated Easter in Kilkeel, County Down that year, while his brother remained in England.

On another Easter holiday, Jack went on one of his beloved walking tours—this time with his friends, Barfield, Griffiths, and a man named Beckett. He and his friends would often hike as much as eighty miles or more over the course of several days. The entire walking journey took them from Eastbourne to Midhurst on the South Downs Way.

Jack's friend Owen Barfield joined him for another walking tour that took the pair across Derbyshire, which Jack described as being more like his ideal type of country than anything he had ever seen. Derbyshire was, to Jack's mind, like the delectable mountains in one of John Bunyan's stories, *Pilgrim's Progress*. At the same time, Jack was saddened by the destruction of the countryside around The Kilns. As a result of the growth of the Morris Motors automobile factory, about a mile from The Kilns, many new houses were being built on the once vacant Kiln Lane. Lewis and Tolkien were both disturbed by the industrialization of Oxford in their lifetime, and their environmental concerns were reflected in their writing.

A NEW FRIEND

In early 1936, Nevill Coghill introduced Jack to a book by Charles Williams. Jack was bowled over by Williams' supernatural thriller *The Place of the Lion*. He immediately wrote to the author, an editor for the Oxford University Press in London. He praised Williams for his great work. Jack called his reading of Williams' book a major literary event, as important as his first discovery of George MacDonald or G. K. Chesterton. Jack invited Williams to attend one of the sessions of the informal literary club, the Inklings, which had grown out of his meetings with Tolkien. In response,

Williams wrote back to Jack thanking him for his new book, *The Allegory of Love*. Williams had been asked to write a review of the book. Furthermore, Williams said that he would very much like to come to Oxford. Thus began a long and very important friendship in Jack Lewis's life.

The 1930s were important years in terms of all the new friends that Jack made. One of the most significant friendships formed, of course, was with J. R. R. Tolkien. At last, there was someone nearby who shared many of Jack's tastes in literature—especially in Norse mythology. Not only that, but Tolkien was a man from whom Jack could learn. "Tollers," as Jack nicknamed him, was shaping Jack's understanding of mythology, especially as it related to Christianity. And Hugo Dyson was another man who was shaping Jack's thoughts on literature, religion and philosophy. These friendships were like a lifeline to Jack. So it should come as no surprise that Jack would say: "If a man has a choice about where to live, he should choose a place where he can be closest to his friends." The full flowering of Jack's thoughts on friendship would eventually appear in his book *The Four Loves*.

ANOTHER WAR ON THE HORIZON

As a potential war between England and Germany was looming on the horizon, Jack was rethinking his view of war from a Christian perspective. Jack came to believe that it was right for a Christian to fight for his country when commanded to do so by his government. It wasn't that Jack liked war; his service in the army during World War I brought him nightmares for the rest of his life. But Jack believed what the Bible and great Christians like Saint Augustine and others down through the ages had taught—war is sometimes a necessary evil. In other words, sometimes the only way to stop great evil is by physical fighting.

In September 1939, the peaceful time which Jack and all his friends had known since the cessation of The Great War was soon to come to an end. The Second World War would bring many unexpected changes to all

THE PROFESSOR OF NARNIA

of their lives. For Jack, it would mean crawling even further out of the shell of his own selfishness. Like Eustace shedding his dragon skin and becoming a real boy again, so, too, Jack was becoming more and more a real man. He was becoming a man whom God could use to help millions of people come to know Jesus Christ in a personal way.

THE CONTINUED WAR AGAINST THE POWERS OF DARKNESS

C.S. Lewis once wrote that *The Silver Chair* was about "the continued war against the powers of darkness." September 1939 was certainly a dark time for the world. On September 1, Germany invaded Poland. Two days later, Britain and France came to Poland's aid by declaring war against Hitler's Germany.

Jack and Warnie Lewis were among the millions of people who joined in this "war against the powers of darkness." One way the Lewis brothers assisted in the war effort was by receiving evacuees in their home. Four schoolgirls from London were evacuated to The Kilns, part of a massive exodus of children from London in anticipation of the German bombing of the city. Jack later used the evacuation of children from London as part of the plot in *The Lion, the Witch and the Wardrobe*.

Warnie, being in the Army Reserve, was called back into service. Soon Warnie began serving with the 6th Oxford City Home Guard Battalion. During the summer months, he offered his "floating" service from his boat, the *Bosphorus*, which he cruised along the rivers of Oxfordshire. At the same time, Jack was serving as a Local Defense Volunteer. In this job, he spent the early hours of every Saturday morning lugging a heavy rifle around the more unattractive parts of Oxford, often with other men who were also serving in the Local Defense.

The Inklings

One good result of the war was that Jack's friend Charles Williams moved to Oxford from London with the Oxford University Press. Thus Jack got to spend time with Williams every week and Williams became a regular part of the Inklings. This group of friends, who were all interested in literature, would meet on Thursday nights in Jack's rooms at Magdalen College. Their meeting on November 11, 1939 was typical. Dinner at the Eastgate Hotel was followed by readings in Jack's rooms, including bits of what the group called *The New Hobbit*, which would become J. R. R. Tolkien's *Lord of the Rings* trilogy. Charles Williams read a Christmas play he was writing and Jack read a chapter out of his new book, *The Problem of Pain*. It must have been quite a literary feast! However, this was no mere mutual admiration society. Each man was unstinting in praise when it was deserved, but none of the group held back in meting out criticism of shoddy work.

While the Inklings devoted Thursday nights to the reading of works in progress, it was not the only time this group of friends got together. They would also meet in the back room of the Eagle and Child pub on St. Giles Street in Oxford every Tuesday morning. You should know that pubs in England are not merely a place for adults to drink. Pubs these days are also very kid-friendly. If you go to a pub in England, sometimes you will find that you can get a very good meal there. Some pubs even have fancy dinners like roast beef and Yorkshire pudding on Sundays! At any rate, if ever you do visit the Eagle and Child, also known as the Bird and Baby, you will see photographs of C.S. Lewis and his friends on the wall, along with a plaque which tells about the Inklings.

Preaching

While the physical war between England and Germany was going on, Jack also realized there was a more important spiritual war underway for the souls of people. One way in which Jack began to fight in the war against spiritual powers of darkness was through preaching. In the autumn of 1939 he preached his first sermon at St. Mary the Virgin, the University Church in Oxford, from the same pulpit where John Wesley once preached. The title of Jack's sermon was *Learning in War-Time*. It was a timely message.

The following year, on a Sunday evening in June, Jack preached another sermon at St. Mary's. This sermon was called *The Weight of Glory*. It was based on the Scripture in which St. Paul says, "For our light and momentary troubles are achieving for us an eternal glory that far outweighs them all" (2 Corinthians 4:17).

You might wonder what the response was to Jack's sermons. Fred Paxford, Jack's gardener, on whom Jack later modeled the character of Puddleglum in *The Silver Chair*, once wrote:

> Mr. Jack should have been a clergyman. He would have made a great parson. When he preached at Quarry Church, it was always packed. He had a full clear voice which could be heard all over the church; and he nearly always brought a bit of humor into the sermons; and people seemed to like this. On a few occasions I had to drive him in to Oxford to preach in St. Mary's. As he always liked to be early, I parked the car and went to the service, and the church was always packed.[18]

BOOKS ABOUT CHRISTIANITY

A second way that Jack began to fight in the war against spiritual powers of darkness was through writing books on different Christian topics. Jack was invited to contribute a volume to a collection of books called The Christian Challenge Series. Jack's contribution was the book already mentioned: *The Problem of Pain*. In that book, Jack sought to answer the question: If a good God created the world, then why is there suffering?

---

18. David Graham, editor, *We Remember C.S. Lewis*, Nashville: Broadman & Holman, 2001, p. 127.

Starting in the autumn of 1939, Jack began to meet weekly with a group of students to share his work in progress on *The Problem of Pain*. Jack would read out to the young people a chapter of his book each week and "pick their brains" about it. Jack wanted to be sure that his book, once completed, made sense, at least to college students.

An idea for another Christian book came to Jack while he was sitting in church one Sunday. (Perhaps it was a boring sermon that day!) Before the service was over, Jack got an idea for writing a series of letters from a senior to a junior devil. The older devil, Screwtape, would teach the younger one, Wormwood, how to tempt his human "patient." Jack hoped that by these letters, readers would be more alert to the wiles of Satan. At first these letters were published weekly in *The Guardian*, a Church of England newspaper.

One young man who was a student at Oxford at the time started collecting Jack's devilish letters from *The Guardian*. This young man was quite pleased to finally meet C.S. Lewis one day in Oxford. He asked Jack how many letters, from one devil to another, there were to be in the end. Jack's reply was, "Thirty-one, something diabolical for each day of the month!"

These thirty-one diabolical letters were eventually published in book form as *The Screwtape Letters*. The book sold well from the very beginning. The first two thousand copies, one of which I have in my library, sold out before publication. The book was reprinted eight times in the second year of publication alone. Since then, it has been translated into many languages and has sold millions of copies around the world. The last time I checked, *The Screwtape Letters* was still on the *Publishers Weekly* Religion Paperback Bestsellers List.

At first, Jack was paid just £2 per letter by *The Guardian*. It was at this point in time that Jack began giving away the money he made on writing religious books. He told *The Guardian* to send his pay to a list of widows and orphans, which he supplied to them. Jack never thought he would have to pay tax on this income. So when he received a letter from the British government telling him how much tax he owed, he was shocked! Jack's friend and lawyer, Owen Barfield, came to the rescue. Barfield helped Jack set up a charitable trust into which two-thirds of his income was thereafter directed. The money in the trust was, in turn, given to countless needy people over the years.

BBC RADIO TALKS

A third avenue for fighting against spiritual powers of darkness was opened up to Jack during World War II. He was invited to give talks over the radio by the British Broadcasting Company. Jack immediately wrote back accepting the invitation and suggested a series of talks on right and wrong. Jack eventually gave four talks over the radio in August 1941. This led to a further series of talks in 1942 on the topic *What Christians Believe*. Later that year, Jack gave yet another series of BBC talks, this time on the topic of *Christian Behavior*. In 1944, Jack gave his final series of BBC talks on Christian faith. Most of these talks were delivered live; in fact, only one recording of Jack's BBC talks on Christianity still survives.[19] It has been said that these talks over BBC radio made Jack's voice the most recognizable in all of Britain during the war, second only to that of Prime Minister Winston Churchill.

Just as Churchill sought to encourage the patriotism and optimism of the British people, Lewis sought through these radio talks to encourage their faith. All of these messages were eventually revised, expanded and collected into the one volume entitled *Mere Christianity*, published in 1952.

One quote from *Mere Christianity* may help you understand why Jack's Broadcast Talks were so interesting. At the end of one of these talks, Jack said,

> *I am trying here to prevent anyone saying the really foolish thing that people often say about Him: "I'm ready to accept Jesus as a great moral teacher, but I don't accept His claim to be God." That is one thing we must not say. A man who was merely a man and said the sort of things Je-*

---

19. If you would like to hear C.S. Lewis's voice you can listen online. Just visit my website: www.willvaus.com/c__s__lewis.

sus said would not be a great moral teacher. He would either be a lunatic—
on a level with the man who says he is a poached egg—or else he would be
the Devil of Hell. You must make your choice. Either this man was, and
is, the Son of God: or else a madman or something worse. You can shut
Him up for a fool, you can spit at Him and kill Him as a demon; or you
can fall at his feet and call Him Lord and God. But let us not come with
any patronising nonsense about His being a great human teacher. He has
not left that open to us. He did not intend to.[20]

RAF Talks

Jack's other great wartime work was in lecturing on Christianity at Royal
Air Force bases across Britain. Jack was invited to do this by the Chaplain-
in-chief of the RAF. The first of these talks was given at the RAF base at
Abingdon in April 1941. In May, Jack wrote to Sister Penelope confessing
his feeling that these first talks were a complete flop. Yet, Jack said, "One
must take comfort in the fact that God once used an ass to convert the
prophet Balaam!" Despite this first apparent failure, Jack's talks became
rather popular at the RAF bases. By the autumn of 1941, Jack was hardly
ever at home for more than three nights at a time. The rest of the time he
was traveling and speaking, making the map of his "missionary journeys"
more complicated than that of the Apostle Paul!

The more popular Jack became as an author, preacher and lecturer,
the more he was invited to travel and speak at churches, universities and
RAF bases all over England. This required Jack to travel by train quite
often since he did not drive a car. Jack often said, "The reason I don't
drive a car is because I can't make it go!" He was no good with mechani-
cal things whatsoever.

On one occasion when Jack was supposed to travel by rail, he had lost
his train ticket. He really was an "absent-minded professor" at times. So

---

20. C.S. Lewis, *Mere Christianity*, New York: Macmillan, 1984, Book II, chapter 3, pp. 55–56.

Jack went to the Oxford train station to see if they could solve his problem. Jack walked up to the window and reported to the ticket sales clerk, "I've lost my train ticket and I need a replacement."

"Do you have proof of purchase?" the sales clerk queried.

"No, I don't," Jack answered honestly.

"Well, you look like a trustworthy bloke," replied the clerk. "Here's a replacement ticket."

Jack took the replacement and immediately handed the ticket back to the clerk. "Now may I have my money back, my good sir?"

The amazing thing is that Jack did get his money back that day! He was apparently a convincing communicator, not only in his teaching, but also in everyday life.

MORE BOOKS!

In the autumn of 1941, Jack was working on a new book, the second in his science fiction trilogy; this one was called *Perelandra*. It is the continuing saga of Dr. Elwin Ransom's interplanetary travels. In this story, Ransom goes to Venus where he is called upon to defeat the evil character Weston. Weston, or the Un-Man as he is known in this story, is trying to tempt the Eve of Venus to fall into sin. Jack wrote to his friend Sister Penelope in November 1941, saying that he had gotten Ransom to Venus and through the first talk with the Eve of that planet. The book was published in 1943 and was dedicated "To some ladies at Wantage." The ladies at Wantage were Sister Penelope's fellow nuns, whom Jack had met in the spring of 1941.

In 1943, Jack was already writing the final book in his Cosmic Trilogy: *That Hideous Strength*. Whereas the setting for *Out of the Silent Planet* was Mars, and *Perelandra* was set on Venus, the setting for *That Hideous Strength* was on Earth. The story is all about the continuing interplanetary battle between good and evil. Ransom is once again on the side of the good, but this time he is battling against the N.I.C.E., the National Institute for Coordinated Experiments. The N.I.C.E. takes over a lovely town and university in the heart of England, but their ultimate goal is to take over the world. Perhaps, of all Jack's books, this one most shows the influence of the "supernatural thrillers" written by his friend Charles Williams.

END OF WAR AND DEATH OF A FRIEND

On May 8, 1945, the European portion of the Second World War officially came to an end. The Inklings planned a victory celebration. However, a personal tragedy interrupted those plans on May 15. It was a Tuesday morning, just before the Inklings were to meet at The Eagle and Child pub in Oxford. Having heard that Charles Williams had been taken ill and was in the Radcliffe Infirmary, Jack went to visit him. He went with a book in hand which he wanted to lend to Williams. Jack expected to take messages from Williams back to the other members of the Inklings. Nothing could have shocked Jack more than to learn that Charles Williams had died that morning. Jack even had difficulty making the other Inklings believe that Williams had died, when he took them the sad news.

Jack later wrote that this loss was the greatest he had ever known in his life up to that time. However, Jack said that nothing more greatly confirmed his belief in life after death than the passing of his friend Charles Williams. He felt sure that Charles had entered eternal life and in the days and months that followed, Jack often felt like Williams was alive and very close to him.

Thankfully, the physical war known as World War II ended in 1945. However, Jack still had many spiritual wars to fight against the powers of darkness. He now, unfortunately, had to fight those battles without the physical companionship of one of his dearest friends.

Coming Out of Underworld

As Jack emerged from World War II, he must have felt like Jill, Eustace, Prince Rilian and Puddleglum when they came out of the Green Witch's underground kingdom. Though he had just lost his best friend, Charles Williams, Jack was glad the war was over. Though the post-war rationing would go on for a number of years, it had to feel good to be back in the light and air and freshness of peacetime again.

Time Magazine

Many good things happened to Jack following the Second World War. Jack's bestselling books and his famous radio talks eventually led to *Time* magazine doing a cover story about him on September 8, 1947. On the cover of *Time*, the drawing of Jack's face was flanked by angel wings on one side and a devil with pitchfork on the other. The caption read:

OXFORD'S C.S. LEWIS

His heresy: Christianity.

The article inside was titled: "Don v. Devil." The magazine article noted that Jack, by that time, had sold over a million copies of his fifteen books.

His twenty-nine BBC talks had gone out to an average of 600,000 listeners with each broadcast. *Time* explored Jack's life story and Christian views in some depth. The article also noted that, outside his own particular circle of Christian friends, Jack was not very well liked by his Oxford colleagues. The other Oxford professors and tutors did not like a teacher of English literature writing on Christian subjects. Maybe Jack's Oxford colleagues were just plain jealous.

Once when Jack was asked how he felt knowing that millions of people were reading his books he replied, "It is best not to think about it." Jack knew the dangers of pride. So I imagine what many people would view as the highlight of Jack's career—being on the cover of *Time*—wasn't highly valued by Jack at all.

LECTURES

Not only was Jack becoming a famous author during the 1940s, he was also becoming a popular lecturer at Oxford. Many students felt that C.S. Lewis was the best lecturer at the university. The proof of this was that Oxford eventually had to give Jack their largest auditorium in order to have room for all the students who wanted to hear his lectures. Why was Jack so popular? Part of the reason was that he developed a style of teaching that was very attractive to students. He often introduced humor into his lectures, which the students loved. Also, Jack would invite students to listen to what he had to say without taking notes. Then he would stop and dictate something specific for students to write down. Then he would invite his audience to simply listen again without taking notes. This saved students the stress of trying to figure out what was essential to record and what was not.

Jack was also conscientious about time management in the delivery of lectures. He would begin lecturing while still walking into the hall, and then he would borrow a watch from a student in the front row so as to time himself. (Jack never wore a watch for the same reason he never drove a car—he couldn't make it go. He would forget to wind it and then have trouble resetting it, so he just refused to wear one!) When Jack was nearing the end of his lecture, he would gather up his papers, hand the borrowed watch back to the student, and finish the lecture just as he strode out the back door!

The lecture hall was not the only place where Oxford students heard Jack speak. During the war, a student by the name of Stella Aldwinckle had formed something called the Socratic Club. Its purpose was to provide a place for debate on Christian topics between Christian and non-Christian scholars. Jack was asked to be President by Miss Aldwinckle. Jack served in that capacity until 1954, often delivering talks himself or responding to those who did.

LETTERS

After publishing *The Screwtape Letters* and giving his famous radio talks over the BBC, Jack began to have more and more letters from fans and from people asking him serious spiritual questions. Now that Warnie was back home and living at The Kilns, he was able to help Jack with his increasing correspondence. Jack paid Warnie a small salary to handle routine letters and type lectures and other short pieces. Warnie performed this service all with two fingers by the "hunt and peck" method of typing. He answered many of the letters without bothering his brother except for a signature. The letters written by Warnie had a different flavor from Jack's. Warnie's letters were much more newsy—mentioning weather, politics and other everyday activities. Warnie had a reference number system for each of the letters he typed for his brother. Based upon the reference numbers typed on these letters, we know that by the early 1950s Warnie was averaging between five and six hundred letters per year for Jack.

PROBLEMS AT HOME

Though many good things happened to Jack after the war, he had some difficulties to deal with, too. First of all, Mrs. Moore's mental and physical health was growing worse. As a result, Jack was less and less able to get away from The Kilns, even for a day at a time. His letters reflect the many times he had to say no to various speaking engagements and other invitations. The one bright spot in a very stressful household situation was Mrs. Moore's daughter, Maureen. She was now married to music teacher Leonard Blake. The Blakes would often come from Great Malvern to relieve Jack of his nursing duties. Whenever Maureen and Leonard could come to help, Jack and Warnie would go to Malvern on holiday. In 1947, that holiday took place from April 4 to 17. Jack and Warnie enjoyed the Easter Communion Service at Malvern Priory. They also enjoyed the discovery of the Unicorn Pub opposite the Foley Arms Hotel, as well as hiking the Malvern Hills. Hugo Dyson even showed up on this vacation and joined in on one of the Lewis brothers' favorite walks—to the British Camp, the remains of an Iron Age hill fort located atop the Herefordshire Beacon in the Malvern Hills.

A second difficulty for Jack had to do with his brother Warren. Warnie had, for some time, suffered from alcoholism. This problem began during his time in military service. Shortly after Jack and Warnie returned from vacation in Malvern, Warnie went off alone on holiday to Ireland. There Warnie fell into another alcoholic binge and he landed in the Convent Hospital of Our Lady of Lourdes in Drogheda, Ireland. The doctor was so concerned about Warnie's condition that the hospital sent a telegram to Jack asking him to come over from England. The silver lining in this cloud was that Jack got an Irish holiday out of the deal and was able to visit Arthur Greeves, whom he had not seen in quite some time. However, the cloud of Warnie's alcoholism did not go away; it was another spiritual and emotional battle Jack had to deal with for the rest of his life.

Over time, Jack's daily care for Mrs. Moore and his worries about Warnie wore down his own health. In June of 1949, Warnie returned from a weekend away at Malvern only to find Jack being shipped off to the Acland Nursing Home in an ambulance. Jack's illness was diagnosed as strep throat. It was treated with shots of penicillin every three hours around the clock. Once Jack was on the mend in the hospital, his doctor and fellow Inkling,

Humphrey Havard, recommended a good, long holiday away from The Kilns. As a result, Jack planned to take a month-long holiday in Ireland starting in July. But by the end of June, Warnie was on an alcoholic binge once again. Jack's longed-for trip to Ireland had to be cancelled. Once Warnie was sober again, all Jack could manage were a few brief jaunts away from The Kilns throughout the summer.

INTO THE WARDROBE

In the midst of all these personal and family problems, Jack began to write a completely different kind of book. This project freed his imagination of sorrow and filled him with great joy. During this time, in the summer of 1948, an American writer by the name of Chad Walsh visited Jack in order to interview him for a book he was writing about Jack's life and work. Jack talked to Walsh of completing a children's book which he had begun in the tradition of author E. Nesbit. Nesbit was the author of some of Jack's favorite children's books like *The Aunt and Amabel*, in which a magic world is entered through a wardrobe in a spare room. Jack's story was apparently the continuation of a book he had begun writing in 1939 when child evacuees from London had come to live at The Kilns.

While Jack was in the middle of writing this story, one of his former students, Roger Lancelyn Green, dined with him at Magdalen College. Afterwards Jack read to Green two chapters from his manuscript. Jack told Green, "Tollers already read my children's story and couldn't stand it. Do you think it is any good?"

Green assured him that the story was very good—maybe even a classic. This encouraged his writing and Jack had the complete story ready for Green to read by the end of the month.

You have probably already guessed that this wonderful children's story was titled *The Lion, the Witch and the Wardrobe*. It was first published in 1950. The book was dedicated to Lucy Barfield, Owen and Maud Barfield's adopted daughter and Jack's goddaughter. It was Maud Barfield's concern about children getting trapped in a wardrobe which led to Jack warning against this in the book. The person selected to illustrate all the Narnia stories was Pauline Baynes. She had done the drawings for Tolkien's *Farmer Giles of Ham*.

What was it that inspired Jack to write this special story for children that eventually led to the whole series called *The Chronicles of Narnia*? As with most of his fiction, *The Lion* began with a picture in Jack's mind—in this case, a picture of a faun carrying an umbrella and parcels in a snowy wood. He had this picture in his mind from the time he was sixteen. Finally, when he was about forty, he decided to make a story out of it. At first, he had very little idea of how the story would go along, but then the great lion Aslan came bounding into it. Jack suffered from nightmares throughout his entire life, and around that time he was having a number of dreams with a lion in them. Thus Jack felt like Aslan came into the first Narnia story of his own accord, and once Aslan came on the scene, he pulled six other stories in with him.

By the summer of 1949, Jack was already at work on a sequel to *The Lion, the Witch and the Wardrobe*. However, the story of Digory, later titled *The Magician's Nephew*, which Jack planned as a sequel, didn't come together in the right way at first, and so Jack set it aside. Jack continued his conversations with Roger Lancelyn Green about the Narnia stories. One day he said to Green, "I am very intrigued by the idea of people being summoned, or pulled by magic, into another world. Maybe I will write a story about that."

By September, this idea had developed into the story which would become *Prince Caspian*. By the end of 1949, the manuscript of this story was complete and sent off to Green for his comments. By February 1950, Jack had completed *Prince Caspian* and *The Voyage of the Dawn Treader*.

Like Jack's other stories, *Prince Caspian* and *The Voyage of the Dawn Treader* both started with pictures in his head. Then Jack set about grouping these pictures together. He often wrote down his ideas for new stories in little notebooks. As an example we have this plot sketch from one of Jack's notebooks:

SHIP. Two children somehow got on board a ship of ancient build. Discover presently that they are sailing in time (backwards): the captain

will bring them to islands. Attack by enemies. Children captured. ...
Various islands (of Odyssey and St Brendan) can be thrown in. Beauty
of the ship the initial spell. To be a very green and pearly story.
PICTURE. A magic picture. One of the children gets through the
frame into the picture and one of the creatures gets out of the picture
into our world. ...
SEQUEL TO L.W.W. The present tyrants to be Men. Intervening
history of Narnia told nominally by the Dwarf but really an abstract
of his story which amounts to telling it in my own person.[21]

As you can tell from this brief plot sketch, Jack didn't always use every idea he wrote down. And the stories often came together in different ways as he added his own deliberate inventions. But in this plot sketch we have the essence of *Prince Caspian* where the present tyrants in Narnia are the Telmarines, who are originally from our world. Also in that story you will remember how Trumpkin the Dwarf tells the Pevensies the intervening history of Narnia between their time and that of Prince Caspian.

We also have in this plot sketch the essence of *The Voyage of the Dawn Treader*, a green and pearly story about a ship of ancient build, which Lucy, Edmund and Eustace manage to get to through a picture in Eustace's house. The plot sketch also reveals two of Jack's sources for this story: *The Odyssey* by Homer and the legend of St. Brendan. According to the legend of St. Brendan the Navigator, he traveled in a little coracle from Ireland to the Isle of the Blessed. Perhaps this is where Jack got the idea for Reepicheep to travel in his coracle to Aslan's country. In real life, St. Brendan carried the good news about Jesus to the Celtic people of Ireland, Wales and Scotland in the sixth century. Common to both *The Odyssey* and the legend of St. Brendan are encounters with sea monsters. Jack, of course, borrowed this element from both stories for inclusion in *The Voyage of the Dawn Treader*.

By the end of 1950, Jack had also written *The Silver Chair* and *The Horse and His Boy*, while also making another start on *The Magician's*

---

21. *Companion & Guide*, p. 403.

Nephew. Jack wrote *The Last Battle* in 1952 and he completed *The Magician's Nephew* last of all. *The Chronicles of Narnia* were released, one each year, from 1950 to 1956.

At first, *The Lion, the Witch and the Wardrobe* didn't sell very well. Apparently some parents and teachers were steering children away from the book, thinking it might be too scary for them. Still, Jack was glad to learn how the children who did read the book enjoyed it, for he enjoyed his own books with childlike glee. He even wrote to one correspondent, telling him that he had fun laying out all his books in the shape of a cathedral. Jack thought of all the Narnia stories as side-chapels, each with their own little altar. Thus he was delighted whenever some child wrote to him telling him that the Narnia stories drew them closer to Christ. In one letter to a young person, Jack wrote, "It makes me, I think, more humble than proud to know that Aslan has allowed me to be the means of making Him more real to you."[22]

In the end, the Narnia tales became Jack's most popular books. To date, the Narnia stories have sold over 100 million copies worldwide and they continue to sell at a rate of over a million copies every year.

By 1950, with the joy that Narnia brought to Jack, he must have felt like he had emerged from Underworld for good. However, as we shall soon see, there were still more physical and spiritual battles ahead for Jack Lewis, the Professor of Narnia.

---

22. *Letters to Children,* p. 75.

12

GOOD, ORDINARY TIMES

In *The Last Battle*, Jill says to Jewel the Unicorn, "Oh, I do hope we can soon settle the Ape and get back to those good, ordinary times. And then I hope they'll go on for ever and ever and ever."[23]

In the early 1950s, Jack must have felt very much like Jill. First he had a difficult battle to face, but then it seemed like the good, ordinary times *were* going to go on forever and ever.

THE DEATH OF MRS. MOORE

The first difficult thing Jack had to deal with began when Mrs. Moore had to be moved to a nursing home in the spring of 1950. The doctor told Jack that his adopted mother would probably require professional care for the rest of her life. To make matters worse, Mrs. Moore was quickly losing her mind. When Warnie visited her in June she handed him a letter, telling him that her daughter Maureen had been killed; when Warnie looked at the paper in his hand, it said nothing of the kind. Despite the many demands on his time, Jack remained faithful to the promise he had made to Paddy Moore thirty-three years before; he had cared for Mrs. Moore as if

---

23. C.S. Lewis, *The Last Battle*, New York: Macmillan, 1973, chapter 8, p. 89.

he were her son and once she was in the nursing home, he visited her every day for the rest of her life.

Mrs. Moore's absence had a positive effect on the atmosphere of The Kilns. Jack found home life more physically comfortable and emotionally happy. However, he was worried as to how he could possibly continue paying the £500 per year it cost for Mrs. Moore to be in the nursing home, especially if she should still be alive in nine more years when he would have to retire from Oxford University.

As it turned out, Jack didn't need to worry. Mrs. Janie King Moore died from a bad case of the flu in January of 1951. She was buried in the Holy Trinity churchyard. Jack was finally free of a burden he had carried for over thirty years.

Surprised by Joy

While Jack was losing one important woman in his life, he was gaining another. At the beginning of 1950, Jack received a letter from Mrs. Joy Gresham of Staatsburg, New York. In a sense, Mrs. Gresham was just one more of Jack's American female correspondents. But in another sense, Joy Gresham stood out from the rest because her letters were both amusing and well written. Joy was a pen friend of Chad Walsh, who had published C.S. Lewis: Apostle to the Skeptics the year before. Joy was Jewish by heritage, and had been atheistic by conviction and Communistic in her politics. However, she had come to faith in Jesus partly through reading Jack's books. In her letters to Jack, she enjoyed debating various subjects even though she often lost those debates. Soon a friendship by mail grew between Jack and Joy.

This pen friendship led to a personal meeting in 1952. On September 24 of that year, Jack had lunch with Joy Gresham and her friend Phyllis Williams at the Eastgate Hotel across the High Street from Magdalen College in Oxford. Joy had come to England for several reasons. Her marriage with her husband, Bill Gresham, was falling apart. On top of that she had been ill and her doctor encouraged her to go away for a time of rest. She also needed quiet time to herself to complete work on her book, *Smoke on the Mountain*, a commentary on the Ten Commandments. But most of all, Joy wanted to meet her spiritual mentor, C.S. Lewis. Joy's cousin, Renée Pierce, was staying back in America with the Greshams and so was able to take care of Joy's sons, David (9) and Douglas (7), during Joy's absence.

Apparently the luncheon on the 24th of September was a success because Jack, in turn, invited Joy and Phyllis to dine with him and his brother in his rooms in Magdalen. Warnie withdrew at the last minute because he was always very shy about meeting new people. So Jack invited his friend George Sayer to take Warnie's place. Though some of Jack's friends at Oxford were put off by Joy's New York brashness, Jack was delighted with her bluntness and her wit.

Jack invited Joy to come again for lunch at Magdalen. This time, Warnie agreed to join them along with some of Jack's professor friends. At first Warnie wasn't sure what to make of this dark-haired woman from the Bronx with her horn-rimmed spectacles and her biting wit. During their first luncheon together, Joy turned to Warnie and asked, "Is there anywhere in this monastic establishment where a lady can relieve herself?" Despite his early fears, Warnie grew to love Joy and greatly enjoy her company.

Apparently nothing about Joy's behavior bothered Jack, for he invited her to spend the Christmas holiday with him and Warnie at The Kilns. Joy joined the Lewis brothers for Christmas turkey, long walks, and trips to their favorite pubs. During the visit, Joy read *English Literature in the Sixteenth Century*, on which Jack was making last-minute corrections. She, in turn, shared *Smoke on the Mountain* with him and he gave suggestions for improvement. At the same time, Jack was working on a book on prayer and finishing up writing *The Last Battle*. On Christmas Day, Jack gave Joy a Christmas present—his copy of George MacDonald's *Diary of an Old Soul* signed by MacDonald himself. Joy, in turn, made a present of *Smoke on the Mountain* to Jack by dedicating her book to him.

A few days before Joy sailed for home in January 1953, she received a letter from her husband Bill. Bill told Joy that he was in love with her cousin Renée and that he wanted a divorce. On that depressing note, Joy left England for the United States.

Upon arriving back home in New York, Joy reluctantly agreed to Bill's request for a divorce. She made plans to take her boys with her and move to England. Her stated reason was that it would be cheaper to live in England on the limited support Bill could afford to give her. But certainly her closest friends knew that she was already in love with C.S. Lewis.

David, Douglas and Joy Gresham set sail for England in November 1953. Douglas celebrated his eighth birthday on board ship. The boys were not thrilled with their first sight of England—the dirty Liverpool docks on a bleak day. However, the Greshams made the best of it. Joy rented an apartment in London near her friend Phyllis Williams and enrolled her boys in Dane Court Preparatory School in Surrey. Then Joy acted on the next most important item on her agenda: visiting Jack.

The Gresham boys were excited about what happened next. Jack invited Joy and her boys to spend December 18–21 at The Kilns. Douglas was especially looking forward to meeting the writer of his favorite books, *The Chronicles of Narnia*. Doug figured the man who created Narnia would be like a tall, handsome knight in shining armor. So he was a little disappointed when, instead, he met a stooped, balding, professorial-looking gentleman with nicotine-stained teeth and a shabby tweed coat. But soon Jack's sense of humor and fun made up for what he lacked in looks and stature.

The visit was a joyous time for all of them. Joy wrote to Bill telling him that the boys were a big success with the Lewis brothers. And Jack spoke positively of the visit to one of his friends. However, Jack was overwhelmed by the energy of these small American boys. When Jack took David and Douglas around Magdalen College, he even led them up the narrow, winding staircase in Magdalen Tower. On the rooftop they had a spectacular view of all Oxford. But as soon as they were back down on the ground, the boys pleaded, "Can we climb to the top again?"

The Greshams' visit to The Kilns was short, but it was the beginning of a bigger relationship in the years to come. And that wasn't the only thing that was about to change in Jack's life—in 1954 he was asked to become the

Professor of Medieval and Renaissance English Literature at Oxford's rival, Cambridge University. It was a position created with him in mind.

MOVE TO CAMBRIDGE

Amazingly, Jack was at first reluctant to accept the job in Cambridge. He was concerned about leaving Warnie behind in Oxford and it didn't seem possible to move his entire household to another city. Tolkien, who helped get the job for Jack in Cambridge, went to Jack and urged him to reconsider. Tollers told Jack, "Setting up a permanent residence in or around Cambridge is not necessary. You can simply stay in rooms at the college during the week and come home to The Kilns on the weekends and holidays." Under these conditions Jack felt he could accept the new job. He wrote to Cambridge University on June 4 accepting the position.

This was a big step up in the world of academia for Jack Lewis. Becoming a professor meant that he would no longer have to give tutorials. He could now focus on lectures and scholarly writing. This new job would mean more pay while allowing Jack to focus on the work he most enjoyed—writing. Many of Jack's Oxford colleagues had not liked the fact that he wrote Christian books. Thus Oxford had never offered him a professorship. But what Oxford had denied, Cambridge now offered on a silver platter.

Since this professorship was completely new it was not, at first, attached to any particular college. Cambridge University, like Oxford, is made up of many colleges. Jack was delighted when Magdalene College, Cambridge offered him a Fellowship and rooms.

Jack's job wasn't the only thing that changed in 1954; so did his relationship with Joy Davidman Gresham, who was officially divorced from William Lindsay Gresham that same year. In the spring of 1954, Jack had helped Joy by paying the tuition, room and board for Joy's sons, David and Douglas, to continue at Dane Court Preparatory School in Surrey. And when the fifth Narnian chronicle, *The Horse and His Boy*, was published in

September, it was dedicated to David and Douglas. Clearly, Jack and the Greshams were becoming very close indeed.

However, the highlight for Jack in the year 1954 had to be his 56th birthday on November 29. On that special day he gave his first lecture at Cambridge entitled *The Great Divide*. The largest lecture room at the university was packed and people coming late had to find seats on the floor. Jack's main theme was how to divide up the major periods in history; he insisted that the great divide was not between the Middle Ages and the Renaissance, but between the early 1800s and our own time. Jack called himself a dinosaur because he felt he belonged much more to this earlier period than he did to the twentieth century. After all, most of his favorite authors had lived hundreds of years before his own time!

At the beginning of 1955, with Joy's help, Jack moved his office from Magdalen College, Oxford to Magdalene College, Cambridge. It is curious to note that the names of both colleges are pronounced "maudlin" despite the difference in spelling. Magdalen, Oxford is much grander than Magdalene, Cambridge. The smaller Magdalene consists of a mixture of Tudor, red brick and light brown stone buildings. It is situated along the opposite side of the gently flowing River Cam, apart from the rest of the university. Jack liked his new home better for a number of reasons. Cambridge was then, and is to this day, much less industrialized than Oxford. There is a green belt around Cambridge that preserves its ancient beauty. But the thing Jack really liked better about Cambridge was that he felt there were more Christians around him there. In fact, the motto of Magdalene College is "keep the faith." That is exactly what Jack continued to do throughout the rest of his life.

Jack's Oxford friends adjusted to his move as best they could. The Inklings moved their meeting at the Eagle and Child pub to Mondays before Jack would catch the train from Oxford to Cambridge. Sometimes they would also visit the Trout Inn in Godstow. After the Inklings meeting, Jack's doctor, Humphrey Havard, and one or two others would accompany Jack to Oxford station or perhaps to Islip station out in the countryside.

They would sit with him in the train until the whistle blew. Jack would make a game of it, trying to keep his friends sitting on the train until it left the station. In fact, sometimes his Oxford friends would ride with him all the way to Cambridge! On those special days they would dine with him at Magdalene, enjoy a long evening of conversation, and then sleep in one of the guest rooms of the college, before returning home the next morning.

Jack's daily schedule at Cambridge was similar to that at Oxford, minus the tutorials. His main job was preparing and giving lectures. Every day Jack would rise early, go for a stroll in the Fellow's Garden, and then attend worship service in the small but quaint college chapel at 8 o'clock. Afterwards, Jack would eat breakfast and then attend to his large amount of letter writing; Warnie still handled Jack's correspondence in Oxford, but Jack had to handle his Cambridge correspondence by himself. If he didn't have to give a lecture in the morning, Jack would use the remaining morning hours to write lectures, work on writing books, or read until lunchtime. If not giving a lecture in the afternoon, he liked to go for a walk somewhere around Cambridge. He was good with a map and soon discovered the best footpaths in the immediate area.

Occasionally, Jack would invite a colleague to join him on a day off and they would start the walk in the morning with a stop at a pub for lunch. Then they would continue their walk in the afternoon, with a pause for tea around 4 o'clock.

One of the loveliest places to take tea near Cambridge is The Orchard tea garden in Grantchester. This establishment was opened in 1897 and has been a popular place among students, teachers and tourists ever since. Afternoon English tea is more than just a drink—it is a meal, often including cucumber sandwiches, scones served with jam and clotted cream, toasted teacakes and other assorted desserts. At The Orchard, one can order one's tea and goodies inside and then, on a bright sunny day, sit outside in the tall grass among the fruit trees.

When Jack returned to college after teatime, there was always more work to be done before going to dinner in hall. After dinner he would enjoy a drink in the Senior Common Room, and then he would return to his room for yet more work. Jack would end the day with tea before bed, often inviting others, both colleagues and undergraduates, to enjoy a cup with him.

Weekends and vacations for Jack were spent at home in Oxford. During his first holiday at home, between Lent and Easter Terms[24] at Cambridge, Jack complained to Joy: "I can't seem to get a good idea for a book!" Joy said, "What about that reworking of the myth of Cupid and Psyche which you have thought about writing for so long?" The next day, Jack wrote the first chapter of what would become *Till We Have Faces*. The book was eventually dedicated to Joy who, in a way, inspired some of Jack's later works.

In August 1955, Joy and her boys made an important move from London to 10 Old High Street, Headington—not far from The Kilns. 10 Old High was a three-bedroom, semi-detached, two-story, red brick house with a rather large garden where Joy could grow flowers, herbs and fruit. Jack had found the house for them and he paid the rent.

Obviously, by this time Jack and Joy were very close friends indeed. At first, Jack was attracted by Joy's mind. Jack had met many smart women in his life, beginning with his own mother. However, Joy was the first woman Jack met who had a brain to match his own. For example, when they played Scrabble together, they played with the letters from four sets of Scrabble games and they allowed the use of words from all known languages—both fictional and real! In addition to a great mind, Joy had a mischievous sense of humor and fun. Jack found this combination irresistible, so once Joy moved into 10 Old High Street, Jack began to visit her every day when he was home from Cambridge.

Around this time Jack published his autobiography entitled *Surprised by Joy*. It was the story of his early life and his journey to faith in Christ. The joke that went around Oxford at the time was this:

"Have you heard what's happened to C.S. Lewis?"

"No."

---

24. Cambridge University has three terms: Michaelmas Term runs from the beginning of October to the end of November or beginning of December; Lent Term runs from mid-January through mid-March; Easter Term begins in mid to late April and ends in mid-June.

"He's been surprised by Joy!"

Joy Davidman Gresham truly was one of the greatest surprises and the greatest joys of Jack's life, second only to the joy of his relationship with Jesus Christ.

In early 1956, Jack and Joy had another surprise: the British government refused to renew Joy's visa. Joy did not want to go back to America and Jack didn't want her to go. She was enjoying her new life in England; she thought the schools were better than in America and she didn't want to take the boys back closer to their father. Joy turned to Jack for advice. Jack could think of only one way that Joy could remain in England.

Thus one day in the spring of 1956, the lifelong bachelor C.S. Lewis had a big surprise for his lifelong bachelor brother....

"Warnie, I have decided to marry Joy," said Jack.

"You have?" Warnie responded quizzically.

"Yes, it seemed like the right thing to do," Jack explained.

"It did?" responded Warnie, still lost in a fog.

"Yes, but don't worry Warnie, I am only marrying Joy as a formality."

"You're marrying Joy only as a formality?"

"Yes, a true marriage is before God, not before some government official. I am going to marry Joy so that she and the boys can go on living in England. However, she will stay at her house and we will remain here at The Kilns. That way, everyone's life will go on the same as usual."

And so C.S. Lewis and Joy Davidman Gresham were married in a civil ceremony at the Oxford Registry Office on April 23, 1956. Jack only told his closest friends about the arrangement.

For a while, it did seem that the lives of the Greshams and the Lewises would go on the same. Joy went on living with her boys at 10 Old High Street. Jack went on with his work at Cambridge, living at The Kilns only on weekends and during holidays. When Jack was at home, he would visit Joy every day, sometimes staying at her house until 11 o'clock at night. It did appear like these good, ordinary times were going to go on forever. But something happened in the autumn of 1956 which reminded Jack that good times often do not last...

13

THE LAST BATTLES

"And then the last battle of the last King of Narnia began."[25]

In his letter to Anne Jenkins, C.S. Lewis said that *The Last Battle* was about the coming of the Antichrist (the Ape), the end of the world and the Last Judgment. We may not be alive in our world when it comes to an end as Tirian was alive in old Narnia when it came to an end. Even so, we all will have our last battles to fight. C.S. Lewis had a number of "last battles" beginning in 1956. They were humble battles compared to Tirian's but they were battles nonetheless.

THE FIRST OF THE LAST BATTLES

Suddenly, one day in October 1956, something happened which changed the lives of the Greshams and the Lewises forever. Joy was walking across the room at 10 Old High Street when her hip gave out. She fell to the floor in extreme pain. Joy was rushed to the Wingfield Hospital. There the doctors explained to Jack, "Joy's problem is cancer. The disease has eaten through her left leg bone. That's why the bone snapped like a dry twig. Joy also has a cancerous lump in her breast." Jack had the difficult job of break-

---

25. *The Last Battle*, chapter 12, p. 129.

ing this news to Joy. As part of her treatment, Joy went through no less than three operations in November 1956.

Jack had a hard time admitting it to himself or to his friends, but he was falling in love with Joy. It was the threat of death which made him recognize his true feelings. Joy had one dying wish: she wanted to be married to Jack in a Christian wedding service. And Jack wanted to honor that desire.

In the midst of this terrible time, Jack heard that one of his former students, an Anglican priest by the name of Peter Bide, had a spiritual gift of healing. He asked Bide to come and lay hands on Joy. When Bide arrived at the hospital and prayed over Joy at her bedside, the subject of marriage was also discussed. Peter Bide quickly agreed to marry them. And so on March 21, 1957, Jack and Joy were married for a second time! They had a bedside Christian wedding ceremony right in the hospital. Their marriage was no longer a mere formality. It was a real marriage before God and the world.

In April, Joy was sent home to The Kilns to die. But once again, there was a surprise in store. By the end of September, Joy's health had improved. Many people considered it a miracle. By November, Joy was even walking around the house and garden with a cane.

Once Joy had sprung back to life, she helped her new home to do the same. In early 1958, she set about painting and repairing The Kilns, which had fallen into a state of almost total neglect over the years. There were holes in the floors, walls and ceilings. Carpets were in tattered rags from Jack and Warnie scattering their cigarette ashes on them for thirty years. Jack's friends referred to The Kilns as "The Midden," an old English word for a rubbish heap; apparently the title was very appropriate. It seemed The Kilns was just a ramshackle house held up by books. Joy was afraid that if they moved the bookshelves the whole place would come crumbling down!

The central heating system, which hadn't worked in ages, was overhauled and put back in working order. Floors, walls and ceilings were repaired. A fresh coat of paint and new carpets did wonders. Blackout curtains from the war were removed and replaced with fine draperies. Joy even bought new china and crystal to complement the delicious meals she served as hostess at The Kilns.

Joy also got Paxford (the gardener, occasional cook, grocery shopper and general handyman around The Kilns) to set the grounds of The Kilns back into shape. "Paxford, do you think we can fix up the vegetable garden and flower beds?" Joy queried.

"I'll see what I can do, mum," Paxford replied.

And so Paxford, a lifelong bachelor who wasn't bothered by taking his orders from women, set about his newly assigned tasks with vigor, bellowing hymns and other tunes, off-key, as he went. The flowerbeds were re-dug and planted, along with the vegetable garden, or "gyaarden" as Paxford would have called it with his Cotswold accent. The falling-apart greenhouse was reconstructed with a new heating system. Once the whole job was done, The Kilns became a paradise to which Jack was happy to invite friends once again.

As Joy began to feel better, she also went on short trips with Jack outside of The Kilns. In January 1958, she went with him back to Cambridge by car for the beginning of the next term. Their driver, Clifford Morris, would also take Jack and Joy out to Studley Priory in Horton-cum-Studley, Oxfordshire for Sunday lunch or afternoon tea. The first time Jack and Joy went away together to stay at a country hotel, Jack, confirmed old bachelor that he was, could hardly believe he was married!

By May 1958, Joy was feeling much better. And so one day Jack asked, "Joy, are you ready for a real holiday?"

"Where to?" Joy asked.

"To the land of my birth," Jack responded. "We shall go to Ireland together!"

Jack and Joy flew to Ireland in a plane, their first experience of air travel. After the initial fright of take-off, they found it enchanting. Peering through the clouds to glimpse the world where he was born was a beautiful experience for Jack. Joy thought Ireland was the greenest place she had ever seen.

The couple stayed at The Old Inn in Crawfordsburn, County Down, not far from Jack's former home outside of Belfast. The Old Inn is a rambling Tudor-style hotel and is, in fact, the oldest inn in Ireland. While in

Ulster, Joy met Arthur Greeves for the first time. Jack and Joy's stay in Crawfordsburn was just one part of a delightful trip which also included visits to Donegal, Louth and the rest of County Down. Jack later wrote to a friend saying that he and Joy returned from Ireland "drunk with blue mountains, yellow beaches, dark fuchsia, breaking waves, braying donkeys, peat-smell, and the heather just then beginning to bloom."

Unfortunately, the delights of these special times were not to last. In October 1959, Jack wrote to various friends pleading, "Redouble your prayers for Joy! The last x-rays have revealed cancerous spots returning to her bones."

1960 was a year of joy, followed by great sadness, for Jack. Even as they feared for Joy's life, she plucked up the courage to ask Jack for one more gift. "Jack, I want to go to Greece. It's been my lifelong dream. Can we do it?"

"Are you feeling up to it, Joy?"

"I'm game if you are!" Joy quickly replied.

In 1959, their friends June and Roger Lancelyn Green had gone on a tour to Greece and come back with a glowing report. Thus the four planned to do a similar trip together, April 3–14, 1960. Their plans were carried out despite the return of Joy's cancer. On their first afternoon in Athens, Jack and Joy were able to climb to the top of the Acropolis. They huffed and puffed but they made it to the top. There they sat on the sun-bleached steps and drank in the magic and mystery of the most famous temple in the world, the Parthenon. From the steps of this ancient temple they could see Mars Hill where the Apostle Paul preached to the Greek philosophers: "Now what you worship as something unknown I am going to proclaim to you" (Acts 17:23).

"Jack, did you ever imagine any place this stunning?" Joy quietly asked her husband.

"No, my love, but being here with you brings the ancient world of Homer alive for me again. I feel like a schoolboy on holiday."

When they returned from their dream trip, Jack wrote to Chad Walsh that it was, from one point of view, a crazy idea. But neither he nor Joy regretted it. He reported to Walsh how Joy climbed the Acropolis, limped up through the Lion Gate of Mycenae, and tramped about the medieval city of Rhodes on the edge of the beautiful, azure blue Aegean Sea. Joy seemed to be supported by God during the trip. She returned home ready to die, if that was God's will.

Joy did return from Greece much weaker; her muscles had been overused. The original cancerous growth in her right breast returned. It was removed in May, and Joy seemed to recover fairly easily from the operation, returning home to The Kilns a fortnight later.

However, in late June, Joy was back in the Acland Nursing Home. Thinking that she was dying, Joy asked the nurse, "Please have my boys brought home from school. I must see them one last time." Doug arrived in tears, having heard the news from his Headmaster, who drove him all the way from Wales to Oxford. However, everyone was fooled once again, and Joy recovered temporarily, returning home to The Kilns.

At the beginning of July, Joy was doing well enough to go to Studley Priory with Jack for their usual Sunday dinner. The next day she even went for a drive in the Cotswolds. A week later, Joy was in good spirits. She and Jack did a crossword puzzle together and played Scrabble. That same evening, they had a long and comforting talk about love and life and death.

However, the next morning Warnie, who slept in the room over Joy, woke to hear his sister-in-law screaming in pain. Jack telephoned the doctor, who arrived by 7 a.m. to give Joy some pain medication. Jack was able to talk Joy's surgeon into giving her a bed in a private ward at the Radcliffe Infirmary. Once she got to the hospital, Joy slept from time to time. During those final hours, she told Jack, "You have made me so happy" and "I'm at peace with God." Joy died around 10:15 that night, Wednesday, July 13, 1960.

Joy's funeral service took place at the Oxford Crematorium where her ashes were later buried. Jack, Warnie, David, Douglas and a few others were present for the service. Unfortunately, none of Jack's friends attended the funeral except for Austin and Kay Farrer. The Farrers were among the few of Jack's friends who had been able to accept Joy's brash, Bronx manner and adjust to the fact that Jack, a lifelong bachelor, suddenly had a woman in his life. Austin, as priest, led Joy's service. However, he was so overcome by sadness that he wept openly as he read the words of the liturgy. It was a windy day full of sunshine; Doug felt that God had given his mother a fine and fitting farewell to this world.

Jack was so overcome by grief that the only way he could get through it was to turn to his best means of coping—writing. In August 1960, he began jotting his thoughts on grief in a diary. Every day he would write something and then read it back to himself. When Roger Lancelyn Green came to visit and learned of Jack's journal, he asked if he might read it. When he did, he realized what a great help Jack's diary might be to others wandering through the winding valley of grief. At first, Jack was reluctant to publish his private journal; the emotions expressed in it were too troubled.

However, Roger convinced Jack to publish his journal under a pen name: N. W. Clerk. And so, A Grief Observed was published a year after Joy's death. Few copies were sold until the book was re-issued under Jack's own name after his death. Curiously enough, some of the people who knew Jack and who read A Grief Observed by N. W. Clerk thought the book would be helpful to Jack. So they sent him copies of his own book, not realizing he was the author!

JACK'S DOWNHILL JOURNEY

Jack continued to write and publish a number of books, but his life was empty without Joy. After her death, he was never the same man again. In June 1961, Arthur Greeves came to visit Jack in Oxford. But Arthur noticed during his visit that Jack was not looking well. After Arthur returned to Belfast, Jack went to see his doctor, Humphrey Havard. Humphrey diagnosed an enlarged prostate gland. He was so concerned about Jack that he immediately booked a room for him in the Acland Nursing Home.

The surgeon at the Acland came to the conclusion that Jack was not well enough to survive an operation on his prostate. Jack's kidneys were infected and poisoning his blood. This, in turn, was causing heart problems. Jack received a number of medicines and was put on a low-calorie, low-protein diet. He had to sleep upright in a chair and could not climb stairs anymore. Jack was told he must quit smoking, but he refused. He had smoked for most of his life and he felt to give it up would make him too irritable. The doctors also told him he could not return to Cambridge for the Michaelmas Term, and he had to have regular blood transfusions. Jack wrote to a colleague at Cambridge, "Dracula must have led a horrid life!"

In April 1962, Jack was allowed by his doctors to return to his work at Cambridge on an experimental basis. George Sayer drove him there one Monday. On the way, they stopped at Woburn Abbey where the Dukes of Bedford have lived for over 350 years. Jack and George entered the woods by a small gate. Walking by a narrow path, they suddenly found themselves in an open field, surrounded by tiny deer. Jack was moved by the magic of it all. He told his friend, "Even while writing the Narnia books, I never imagined anything so beautiful."

THE LAST YEAR

For many years Jack had tried to write a book on prayer, but it never came together the way he would have liked. Then, at the end of 1962, Jack had a great idea: Why not write a book on prayer in the form of fictitious letters to a friend? That is exactly what he did. He named the friend Malcolm and so the book was called: *Letters to Malcolm: Chiefly on Prayer*. This format enabled Jack to say what he wanted about prayer without sounding too preachy.

Unfortunately, Jack continued to have health problems in early 1963. He had a bad night in mid-January; he woke in the middle of the night and was in need of a doctor. Warnie was away and so Jack had no one to help him. He called for an ambulance. However, the ambulance was not able to get up the driveway to The Kilns due to snow. Jack had to walk down to Kiln Lane in the freezing cold and wait for the ambulance at 2 o'clock in the morning. Even so, he enjoyed the full moonlight on the wintry landscape and he was back in bed at The Kilns a few hours later.

Despite his health problems, Jack was able to return to Cambridge for the Lent and Easter Terms of 1963. Friends who saw him then said he was as happy and funny as ever. The Inklings continued to meet, though not at The Eagle and Child pub. In 1963, they had to move across the street to The Lamb and Flag. But they continued to see Jack off to Cambridge every Monday afternoon in term time.

In June, Jack returned from Cambridge to The Kilns for summer vacation. Warnie had gone off to Ireland for a long holiday, and so Jack was alone on June 7 when he had a young man from North Carolina join him for tea. The man's name was Walter Hooper and he had been writing letters to Jack since 1954. The two met together many times in the weeks which followed, and Jack eventually asked Hooper to help him with his letter writing while Warnie was away on his Irish jaunt.

In July, Jack's ankles began to swell up again—a danger sign showing that his kidneys were not working right. Sadly, Jack had to cancel a planned trip to Ireland with his stepson Douglas. Jack went into the Acland Nursing Home for an examination. While there, he had a heart attack and went into a coma for almost twenty-four hours; he was able to breathe only by means of an oxygen mask. The doctors told Austin and Kay Farrer that they thought Jack was dying. But to everyone's surprise, at 3 p.m. Jack woke from the coma. "May I have my tea, please?" Jack asked the nurse.

In the weeks which followed, Jack had hallucinations and was generally not himself. But after three weeks in hospital, he regained his right mind and, slowly, his physical strength. At the beginning of August, he returned home to The Kilns with Walter Hooper and a nurse, Alec Ross, to look after him.

One of the first things Jack did upon arrival at The Kilns was to write to Cambridge and resign his job as professor. Jack knew he would never be well enough again to return to work there. Jack said to Walter, "Would you mind going to Cambridge and packing up my books and things? Take Douglas along. He can help you. Doug is a real brick, you know." After that job was done, Walter returned to the United States; he had to teach one more semester at the University of Kentucky before returning to Oxford to continue helping Jack as his secretary.

Warnie returned to The Kilns in the second half of September. By early October, it was clear to both of them that Jack was going to die soon. But their last days together were not without some happiness. It was as if life had come full circle. The two brothers were alone together. David had gone off to school in America. Doug was away at school in England. It was as if Jack and Warnie were together again in the Little End Room, just as they had been at the beginning of their lives. They were enjoying the last moments of their holiday as they had learned to do as schoolboys.

Jack faced his own death bravely and calmly; he almost looked forward to it. He wrote to a correspondent at the end of September saying that autumn was really the best of the seasons and that, perhaps, old age was the best part of life. But like autumn, old age doesn't last. Jack told his beloved brother, "I've done everything I wanted to do. I'm ready to go."

Friday, November 22, 1963 began like any other day for Clive Staples Lewis: breakfast, followed by letter writing and then the crossword puzzle. After lunch, Jack fell asleep in his chair. Warnie suggested he might like to move to his bed. At four o'clock, Warnie took tea in to his brother's bedroom. They talked very briefly. Then at 5:30, Warnie heard a crash and ran in to find Jack on the floor at the foot of his bed. A few moments later, Jack Lewis breathed his last. The news of Jack's death was overshadowed by the death of another Jack on that same day: American President John F. Kennedy was assassinated in Dallas, Texas.

Jack Lewis's funeral took place on Tuesday, November 26. He was buried in the churchyard at Holy Trinity, Headington Quarry—a short walk from The Kilns. A small group of Jack's friends were present at the funeral. Doug was the one representative of the family. Warnie did not have the emotional strength to handle being present at his brother's funeral. But later, Warnie had engraved on Jack's gravestone the words which appeared on the family calendar the day of their mother's death: "Men must endure their going hence."

14

THE TITLE PAGE

And for us this is the end of all the stories, and we can most truly say that they all lived happily ever after. But for them it was only the beginning of the real story. All their life in this world and all their adventures in Narnia had only been the cover and the title page: now at last they were beginning Chapter One of the Great Story, which no one on earth has read: which goes on for ever: in which every chapter is better than the one before.[26]

November 22, 1963 was the beginning of the real story for Jack Lewis. Only Aslan knows how that story is going on and what Jack is doing right now in the new Narnia. But concerning Jack's life in our world we can say this: since 1963, more books have been written about C.S. Lewis and his works than the 40-plus books he wrote during his sixty-five years on planet Earth. Today there are over 200 million copies of Jack's books in print, making C.S. Lewis the best-selling Christian author of all time. It has been said that, after Jesus Christ and the Apostle Paul, C.S. Lewis is one of the most quoted spokesmen for Christianity. By almost any measure, Clive Staples Lewis was a remarkable human being.

However, probably very few people ever would have heard of C.S. Lewis had it not been for the joy that surprised him on that journey to

---

26. *The Last Battle*, chapter 16, p. 184.

Whipsnade Zoo in September 1931. If it was not for that day when Jack returned to faith in Jesus as God's Son, he never would have written at least half of the books that he wrote, including the Narnia stories. For as Jack told Anne Jenkins: "The whole Narnian story is about Christ."

I'm sure you will remember that at the end of *The Voyage of the Dawn Treader*, Aslan says to Lucy, "This was the very reason why you were brought to Narnia, that by knowing me here for a little, you may know me better there."[27] Perhaps that is why you were brought to read the Narnia stories, so that by getting to know Aslan for a little while there, you might get to know him better in this world. But in this world he goes by another name. You have probably figured out by now that Aslan's name in this world is Jesus.

One way you can get to know Aslan better in this world is by reading a book which is like Coriakin's book in *The Voyage of the Dawn Treader*. You may remember Coriakin's magic book in which Lucy reads a story which refreshes her spirit. We have a book just like that in our own world. The book I am talking about was, in many ways, Jack's favorite book out of all the hundreds of books he read during his lifetime. It is a book which he read every day during the second half of his life—the wonderful collection of books known as the Bible. For the Bible contains the greatest story ever told, the story of Jesus' death on the cross for traitors like you and me, and his resurrection from the dead. It is a story very much like the story of Aslan in *The Lion, the Witch and the Wardrobe*. When you read the Bible every day you will find it refreshing your spirit and drawing you closer to the real Aslan.

Another way you can get to know Aslan better in our world is by talking to him. You might ask, "How can I do that?" I am sure Aslan would like you to address him by his proper name in our world—that is, Jesus. And you can talk to him in prayer. Perhaps the most important prayer anyone can ever pray goes something like this:

Dear Jesus, I agree with You that I am a sinner, a traitor just like Edmund. I believe that You died on the cross for my sins. I believe You rose

---

27. C.S. Lewis, *The Voyage of the Dawn Treader*, New York: Macmillan, 1973, chapter 16, p. 216.

again from the dead. I believe You are the Son of God. Please come into
my heart by Your Holy Spirit and help me from this day forward to follow
You, along with other believers in Your kingdom.

If you sincerely pray that prayer right now, today can be the title page of eternity for you. You see, eternal life is not something which begins after you die. Eternal life can begin in your heart the moment you accept Jesus as your leader and forgiver, just like Jack did on that motorcycle journey to Whipsnade Zoo.

If you are beginning a personal relationship with Jesus Christ I would love to hear from you and encourage you in your journey. You may write to me at my e-mail address: will@willvaus.com or visit my website any time you want: www.willvaus.com.

Until I hear from you or until we meet—enjoy the journey further up and further in!

RECOMMENDED READING

I thought you might like to have some ideas of what other books you can read by or about C.S. Lewis. So I will tell you what books I have most enjoyed, which will start you out on a good footing for the rest of your journey with Jack.

If you are especially interested in the stories Jack wrote as a child, I am happy to tell you that many of these stories, along with the pictures Jack drew, have been published in a book. That book is called *Boxen*, of course! Walter Hooper, the editor of that book, will tell you many things you might like to know about Jack's first stories.

If you would like to see more photographs of C.S. Lewis's England and Ireland, I would highly recommend buying Douglas Gilbert and Clyde Kilby's book *C.S. Lewis: Images of His World*. It is a beautiful book you can enjoy at any age. When I was in college, this book whetted my appetite for the places I eventually visited on the C.S. Lewis pilgrimage I took in 1982.

Another wonderful book, filled with lovely photographs and stories from Jack's childhood, is Ruth James Cording's book *C.S. Lewis: a Celebration of his Early Life*. You will enjoy reading this little book no matter what age you are.

When I was in middle school, my Aunt Helen gave me a book which I have treasured for many years. The title is *The Joyful Christian* and it contains 127 little snippets from many of C.S. Lewis's books. Reading this book would be a great way for you to be introduced to Jack's writings beyond Narnia.

When I graduated from college, one of the best friends I have ever had, Megan McLeod, gave me a book called: *C.S. Lewis: Letters to Children*. I wish that this book had been published when I was ten years old, as I would have read it and loved it. It is a book filled with letters Jack penned to his godchildren and to children from all over the world who wrote to him about his Narnia stories. When you read this book you will feel like Jack is talking directly to you.

In high school, I began to read some of Jack's books beyond Narnia. If fiction is what you like best, you might want to start with Jack's science fiction trilogy, beginning with *Out of the Silent Planet*. Other fictional works you might want to read if you are in high school would include *The Screwtape Letters* and *The Great Divorce*.

When I went on my trip to England and Ireland in 1982, I read many of C.S. Lewis's books for the first time. *Mere Christianity*, *Miracles* and *Till We Have Faces* were among the books I read at that time. If you are in college or older you may be ready to read these books, along with *The Problem of Pain*, *The Weight of Glory*, and *The Abolition of Man*.

These are just a few suggestions for your journey with C.S. Lewis. For a complete listing of Jack's books in print you may visit my website: www.willvaus.com/c__s__lewis_store.

ACKNOWLEDGEMENTS

I could not have written this book without the resources of many fine earlier biographies on C.S. Lewis. Of course, I have drawn heavily on Jack's autobiography, *Surprised by Joy*, but it only covers the first half of his life. I am also indebted to George Sayer for his excellent biography, *Jack: a Life of C.S. Lewis*. I think Sayer's work is the best of the complete biographies of Lewis on the market. I am also grateful for the personal reflections on the life of C.S. Lewis written by Jack's stepson, Douglas Gresham. I have been greatly helped in my Lewis studies by Doug's two books: *Lenten Lands* and *Jack's Life*. Both versions of the movie *Shadowlands*, about Jack's relationship with Joy Davidman Gresham, have also given me, and many others, an interesting picture of what Jack's life in the 1950s looked like.

One of the greatest gifts to Lewis studies is Walter Hooper's huge work: *The Collected Letters of C.S. Lewis*. I am sure you will be amazed if you ever read this three-volume collection. It is thousands of pages long and contains hundreds of letters Jack wrote over his lifetime. Another very helpful volume written by Walter Hooper is *C.S. Lewis: Companion & Guide*. I often turned to this guide in the course of writing this book. It answers almost any question a Lewis fan could have about Jack's life and work.

I have been reading books by and about Jack for so long, as well as talking to people who knew him, that I often forget where I first read a certain story or heard a little tidbit. However, if you would like a detailed tracing of these stories of Jack's life back to the original sources, I would suggest reading my biographical essays on C.S. Lewis contained in the excellent collection, *C.S. Lewis: Life, Works, and Legacy, Volume I: An Examined Life*, edited by Bruce Edwards. Although the $300 price tag to purchase all four volumes of this encyclopedic collection may place too much of a strain on your wallet, these collected essays by Lewis scholars from around the world may be consulted in many libraries.

I am most grateful to my publisher, Believe Books, for the top-notch work they do making the inspirational life stories of notable Christ-followers available to the world. Without Christian biographies, where would the Church be? Such stories have been essential to the life and growth of the Church as well as individual Christians ever since Dr. Luke first set pen to paper and told us the transforming life story of the Apostle Paul. Though this little book doesn't rank in the same category, I am thankful to Believe Books for making it available to the general public.

I wish to acknowledge and thank my family for their invaluable help in listening to and commenting on each chapter of this book as I wrote it. My three sons, James, Jonathan and Joshua, consistently brought me back to reality. They reminded me of what was really of interest to children and youth, and what was not. The looks on their faces as I read this book aloud to them told me whether I was getting it right or not! And without the constant encouragement of my wife, Becky, I would find it much more difficult to get through life from day to day. She makes the sad times easier to bear and the happy times sweeter than I deserve.

Of course, I must also give praise to the God who called C.S. Lewis into His kingdom. As St. Paul wrote, quoting a Greek poet, "In Him we live and move and have our being" (Acts 17:28). Truly, apart from Jesus I could do nothing. To my one Lord—Father, Son, and Holy Spirit—I give all the glory.

And one last thing: a note to you as the reader and to the subject of this book. Please be aware, reader, that much of the dialogue written in this book is the result of my own historical imagination. And to the subject: I hope you don't mind, Jack, if I put a few words on your lips here or there! If you do mind, I'm sure you will forgive me when we meet some day....

Mary Haskett

REVEREND MOTHER'S DAUGHTER

A Real Life Story

In this gripping account, the author shares her personal story of racial rejection, physical and sexual abuse, and wartime trauma. Through it all, she is aware of a driving force in her life that ultimately brings her to Jesus Christ.

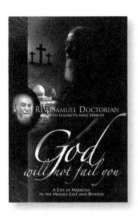

Rev. Samuel Doctorian
with Elizabeth Moll Stalcup, Ph.D.

GOD WILL NOT FAIL YOU

*A Life of Miracles in the Middle East
and Beyond*

The miraculous life story of Rev. Samuel Doctorian, the renowned evangelist used mightily by God in the Middle East and around the world.

Fern C. Willner

WHEN FAITH IS ENOUGH

*A Safari of Destiny that Reveals
Principles to Live By*

A faith-inspiring story of a missionary wife and mother of seven relying completely on God in the heart of Africa.

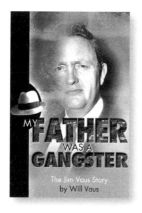

Will Vaus

MY FATHER WAS A GANGSTER

The Jim Vaus Story

One of the most fascinating conversion stories of the 20th century—the dramatic life story of Jim Vaus, former associate to America's underworld.

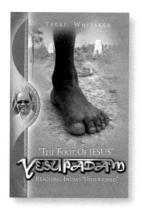

Terri Whitaker

YESUPADAM

Reaching India's Untouched

Yesupadam is the amazing story of God's miraculous work through an Untouchable Indian believer in Jesus and his Love-n-Care ministry in eastern India.

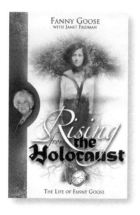

Fanny Goose
with Janet Fridman

RISING FROM THE HOLOCAUST

The Life of Fanny Goose

The astonishing real life story of an indomitable young Jewish girl who miraculously survives the horrors of Hitler's plot to destroy her people and goes on to live a joyful life.

Major General Jerry R. Curry

FROM PRIVATE TO GENERAL

An African American Soldier
Rises Through the Ranks

Major General Jerry Curry vividly describes his life journey of military missions, powerful positions, and his relationship with the true source of authority—his Father in heaven.

Charlene Curry

THE GENERAL'S LADY

God's Faithfulness to a Military Spouse

Charlene Curry recounts all the joys and challenges of being a career military spouse and how she triumphed over difficulties by relying on a source of spiritual power that transformed her life.

Also available from Believe Books:

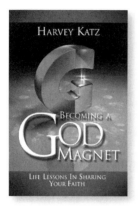

Harvey Katz

BECOMING A GOD MAGNET
Life Lessons In Sharing Your Faith
Book and **Study & Discussion Guide**

Harvey Katz's book *Becoming a God Magnet* is
a practical, effective guide to evangelism. The
Study & Discussion Guide is ideal for church or
home groups willing to learn and share successful methods of personal evangelism.

Howard Katz

SEVEN ESSENTIAL RELATIONSHIPS
How To Pass God's Crucial Tests

The author uses the seven stages in the
creation of a clay vessel, as well as an exposi-
tion of the life of Joseph, to illustrate each
of the seven crucial tests that every believer
must pass.